THE UNDERGROUND RAILROAD

THE HISTORY SMASHERS SERIES

The Mayflower

Women's Right to Vote

Pearl Harbor

The Titanic

The American Revolution

Plagues and Pandemics

The Underground Railroad

THE UNDERGROUND RAILROAD

KATE MESSNER
AND GWENDOLYN HOOKS

ILLUSTRATED BY DAMON SMYTH

RANDOM HOUSE 🏠 NEW YORK

Visit us on the Web! rhcbooks.com

Educators and librarians, for a variety of teaching tools, visit us at
RHTeachersLibrarians.com

Library of Congress Cataloging-in-Publication Data is available upon request.
ISBN 978-0-593-42893-1 (trade)—ISBN 978-0-593-42894-8 (lib. bdg.)—
ISBN 978-0-593-42895-5 (ebook)

Printed in the United States of America
10 9 8 7 6 5 4 3 2 1
First Edition

*For Sarah McCarty and
her sixth-grade SMS readers*

CONTENTS

You've probably heard stories about the Underground Railroad, the secret network of helpers who provided aid to people escaping from slavery. Tales from this chapter of American history are often full of excitement, with freedom seekers racing through the darkness, lanterns hung in windows, and hidden rooms with sneaky getaway tunnels. Maybe you've read about Harriet Tubman, who escaped from slavery and then led hundreds of others to do the same. Or Quaker families who risked everything to help, breaking laws they knew were unjust.

But only some of those stories are true. People really did escape from slavery. In the first half of the nineteenth century, thousands found their way to freedom every year. And some of them did get help, but not from a super-organized national group that provided detailed maps of safe houses. Instead, they found shelter with people who were part of loosely connected antislavery networks, or they got unexpected aid from people who weren't associated with those groups at all. Some of the most heroic helpers were left out of history books entirely, while others claimed more credit than they deserved. And most people who escaped from slavery had to do it on their own, with courage, cleverness, and determination.

The true story of the Underground Railroad involves a lot more than nighttime escapes and secret rooms. It's a story of resistance and resilience—one that begins even before the first enslaved people were brought to the Americas.

ONE
HOW SLAVERY
CAME TO AMERICA

A true history of slavery and resistance begins with the story of the people who were enslaved. Before Africans were taken to the Americas, they lived rich and varied lives as citizens of many different nations. They crafted tools and weapons out of iron and made clothing from the woven fibers of palm leaves. Those who lived near the ocean fished and made salt by boiling seawater in clay jars.

Other African people were farmers. They grew rice, yams, and a kind of grain called millet. They raised oxen, cows, horses, pigs, goats, and dogs. They brought their crops and animals to huge markets,

3

where thousands of people came to find the goods their families needed.

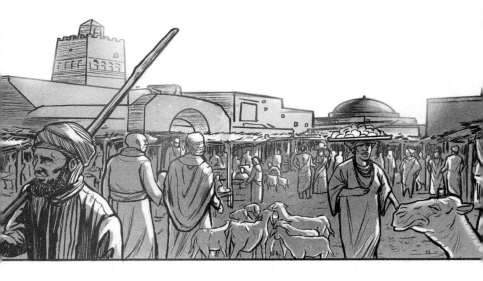

Africa had vibrant economies and organized governments. Even in big kingdoms, many people were involved in decision-making. The kingdoms of Africa had figured out a thing or two about democracy before the United States of America was even a thought, much less a nation on a map.

All that time, African people were making art and developing scientific ideas. They built several great, huge libraries and passed down knowledge from generation to generation. Researchers have rediscovered thousands of ancient African manuscripts, focused on everything from religion to mathematics to astronomy.

Slavery was also part of life in Africa, and that comes as a surprise to some people. But America didn't invent slavery. The practice goes all the way back to ancient Greece and Rome, and Africa, too. Historically, people hadn't been enslaved based on the color of their skin. In ancient times, slavery was most often a way to take advantage of those who had been captured during war.

An ancient Roman mosaic shows
two enslaved men pouring wine.

That began to change in the 1400s, when Portugal started bringing enslaved people from Africa to Europe. You might be wondering how anyone could justify stealing people away from their homes and forcing them to work on another continent, even way back then. Europeans tried to justify it by claiming that African people were inferior to people from Europe.

A Portuguese writer likely helped that idea along. Gomes Eanes de Zurara was a royal chronicler, which meant he was in charge of writing the official history of his nation. He wrote that African people were living "like beasts, without any custom of reasonable beings." He said that if people weren't living peacefully under a government with laws, they really weren't people at all, so it was fine to enslave them.

We know none of that was true. African people had kingdoms and thriving economies, along with great knowledge of science, math, and architecture. Many people in Europe certainly knew that, too. But the racist idea that Africans were somehow inferior took hold. Other Europeans wrote similar things. For centuries, the works of Europeans erased the real history of African people and replaced it with one that would justify their enslavement.

At first, this new slave trade mostly brought African people to Portugal and Spain. Then Christopher Columbus came along.

There are enough myths about Columbus to fill an entire book, but for now, it's enough to know that his explorations opened the door on a whole new era of enslavement. At first, Columbus was sending enslaved people from the Caribbean back to Europe. These were Taino men and women he'd captured from the islands where they'd lived their whole lives.

The Spanish enslaved Native people and forced them to work in the Caribbean, too, in gold mines on the island of Hispaniola.

When those early European explorers arrived in the Americas, they brought along diseases. Native people had no immunity to the new germs, so smallpox and other illnesses ravaged Hispaniola. Less than twenty years after the arrival of Columbus, the Native population had dropped from as many as three million to just about twenty-five thousand who were still able to work.

That's when the Spanish began bringing enslaved people across the ocean, a practice that was marked by cruelty and brutality at every stage. In 1510, King Ferdinand II gave his approval for fifty enslaved African people to be sent from Spain to Hispaniola to work in the gold mines.

... THE BEST AND STRONGEST AVAILABLE!

Three weeks later, the king ordered another two hundred enslaved people to be shipped across the sea under cramped, filthy conditions and forced to work in the mines. This was the beginning of the Atlantic slave trade. Soon slave traders would begin capturing people in Africa and taking them straight to the Caribbean. Over the next 350 years, 12.5 million African people were sold into slavery in the Americas.

THE STORY OF HANDSOME JOHN

You might assume that every Black person who traveled to the Americas was enslaved, but that wasn't the case. Some came as free men, like Juan Garrido, who set sail for the Caribbean on a Spanish ship in the early 1500s, when he was just fifteen years old. Garrido's nickname was Handsome John. (We don't have any pictures of him from that time period, so you'll have to imagine him to decide if the name fit.)

It's not clear how Garrido ended up joining the Spanish. Some historians think he may have been the son of an African king who gave him the job of doing business with the Europeans. It's also possible that he was enslaved and joined the Spanish soldiers in exchange for freedom.

Garrido spent six years in Hispaniola before he went with explorer Juan Ponce de León on a mission to search for gold. They traveled to Puerto Rico and later landed on the peninsula we now call Florida. They claimed it for Spain, but the Calusa people, whose ancestors had lived there for thousands of years, forced them to leave.

Garrido also sailed with Hernán Cortés, a Spanish conquistador, or conqueror, who invaded Mexico and attacked the Aztec people in 1519. Later, Garrido returned to Florida with Ponce de León and a couple hundred settlers, hoping to set up a colony. Native people fought them off again, this time fatally wounding Ponce de León. Garrido escaped and continued to serve with the Spanish.

The slave trade grew so quickly that part of West Africa became known as the Slave Coast: a two-hundred-mile-long stretch that included the modern-day nations of Togo, Benin, and Nigeria. African rulers and merchants made deals with slave traders, sometimes selling their own people into slavery across the sea. The trade increased with the growth of the sugar industry in Brazil and the Caribbean. Sugar plantations required a lot of labor.

As the slave trade grew, the Dutch and the English were also colonizing North America, invading lands that had been home to Native people for generations. They wanted free labor, and merchants eager to make money jumped at the chance to provide it. By 1740, Great Britain was sending more than thirty slave ships to Africa each year, enslaving tens of thousands of people and forcing them on a nightmare journey across the sea.

THE POWER OF WORDS

One of the ways white Europeans and Americans tried to justify slavery was by dehumanizing the people they enslaved, talking about them as if they weren't people at all. Fugitive slave advertisements and other documents written by enslavers refer to the people they enslaved as

SLAVES

ENSLAVED

everything from "beasts" to "creatures" to "slaves." Almost never as people.

But they were people. So in this book, unless we're using the word "slave" as historical language in a quote from a primary source, that's how we'll talk about them, as people. They were not slaves. They were people who were enslaved.

We'll also avoid using the words "runaway" and "fugitive" to describe those who escaped from slavery. Those words make people sound like criminals simply because they rejected the idea that it was fine for one person to own another. "Freedom seekers" feels like a more appropriate choice of words, so that's what you'll find in this book unless it's a quote or another reference from that time period.

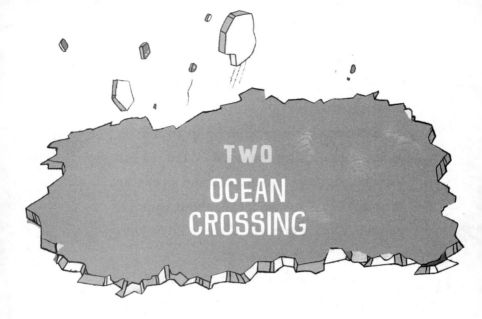

TWO
OCEAN
CROSSING

Today, it's possible to fly from one side of the world to the other in less than a day, but enslaved people who were ripped from their homes were forced to make that journey on ships. It could take over two months to make this harrowing voyage across the Atlantic Ocean, known as the Middle Passage. It was called that because it was the middle leg of the ship's triangular route from Europe to Africa to the Americas, and back to Europe.

All that time, people were packed into quarters so tight that many died of disease along the way. It's estimated that about 1.8 million enslaved people

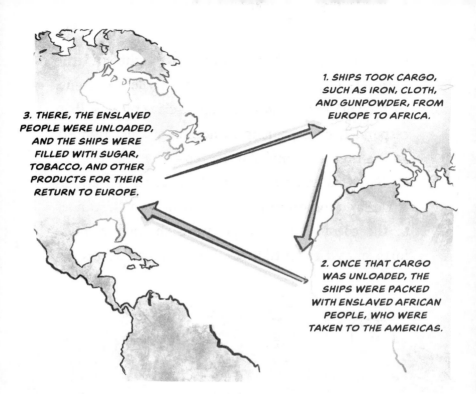

1. SHIPS TOOK CARGO, SUCH AS IRON, CLOTH, AND GUNPOWDER, FROM EUROPE TO AFRICA.

3. THERE, THE ENSLAVED PEOPLE WERE UNLOADED, AND THE SHIPS WERE FILLED WITH SUGAR, TOBACCO, AND OTHER PRODUCTS FOR THEIR RETURN TO EUROPE.

2. ONCE THAT CARGO WAS UNLOADED, THE SHIPS WERE PACKED WITH ENSLAVED AFRICAN PEOPLE, WHO WERE TAKEN TO THE AMERICAS.

died during Middle Passage crossings. Still more died in their first year of forced labor in the Americas.

Enslaved people endured weeks of suffering before they even boarded those ships. Many went from being free people to captives in an instant. How did it happen?

Sometimes, people were enslaved when they lost battles. In 1794, two groups of men from Africa's Gola and Ibau kingdoms had ventured into disputed territory to hunt. The two groups fought, and the king of Gola later raised an army to invade Ibau lands. He took prisoners and sold them to slave traders. Ibau responded by capturing hundreds of Gola fighters and selling them into slavery, too.

Slave traders marched their captives overland in Africa and sometimes traveled down rivers in canoes to the coast. There, people were chained in huge forts, or castles, until it was time to board a ship.

You've probably heard stories about people escaping from slavery in America, but the truth is, enslaved people began fighting back much earlier than that. Some tried to get away before they were loaded onto the ships that would carry them across the sea.

William Butterworth, who worked on a slave ship when he was a teenager, later published a book about what he'd seen. He described enslaved women attacking their captors and leaping from canoes in an attempt to escape.

Those who were forced onto slave ships began a hideous journey. Enslaved people were chained together, packed into the stuffy, cramped space belowdecks. They'd been stolen from different parts of Africa, and singing on the ship helped them find people from their own villages. Then they could communicate in a language the captain and crew didn't understand. Singing also became a way to tell the story of the terrible thing that was happening to them.

Even those who spoke different languages found ways to communicate. Many had already figured out how to understand one another, for trade and other purposes. They used signs and gestures. Some picked up English while they were on board the ships. Communicating with one another enabled captive people to share information about conditions on the ship and how they were being treated.

Sometimes they passed messages to different parts of the ship to plan revolts. Even though they'd been brutally captured and chained, enslaved people were anything but passive. Many were brave warriors with experience in battle. Some knew about Europeans or had worked on ships before. Once in a while they were able to overcome their captors.

IN 1729, A SLAVE SHIP CALLED THE CLARE HAD JUST LEFT THE GOLD COAST OF AFRICA WHEN THE ENSLAVED PEOPLE REVOLTED.

THEY ROSE UP AND TOOK CONTROL OF THE SHIP.

Preparing for a revolt required communication and patience; enslaved people had to wait for just the right moment to strike. African women were often at the heart of this planning. Slave ship captains and crew members tended to underestimate how smart and powerful the women were, so they had more freedom to move around the ship. In 1783, enslaved women on board the *Wasp* attacked the ship's captain and tried to throw him overboard.

Even children rose up against their enslavers. In 1773, when a slave ship called the *New Britannia* was anchored in Gambia, some boys managed to sneak tools to the men chained belowdecks. Enslaved people knew that attempting an uprising was a huge and deadly risk. But conditions on the ship were intolerable, so it was a risk worth taking.

With tools in hand, the men of the *New Britannia* freed themselves, ripped up the lower deck, and seized control of the ship's guns and powder. They battled the ship's crew for over an hour and eventually set fire to the gunpowder storage area, sparking a huge explosion that killed almost everyone aboard the ship.

Once in a while, enslaved people seized control of a slave ship and forced it to return to Africa. But usually, crews were able to quash revolts, and punishments were harsh. Most enslaved people found themselves trapped in floating prisons.

It may be hard to imagine a world where most people thought this was all just fine, but there was no widespread opposition to slavery at that time. Wealthy, powerful men were involved in the cruel practice, and hardly anyone criticized them. Humphry Morice, one of the top slave traders in London in the early 1800s, was a member of the British Parliament. And one of America's busiest slave traders, Henry Laurens, had served as president of the Continental Congress.

LAWMAKERS AND ENSLAVERS

Humphry Morice   Henry Laurens

But not everyone involved in the slave trade was able to ignore its horrors. Some crew members were haunted by their role in enslaving people and spoke up about the horrific conditions on ships. A man named Thomas Clarkson wanted to show people how awful the Middle Passage was, so he traveled to English port cities in 1787 to do research on the slave trade. Clarkson was an abolitionist, someone fighting to get rid of slavery entirely. Merchants and captains involved in the slave trade refused to talk with him, so Clarkson interviewed common sailors, and they told him the real deal about how slave ships worked.

Based on what Clarkson learned, an abolition group created this broadside, or poster, showing how enslaved people were packed into the ships that sailed across the Atlantic.

The illustration was based on real dimensions from a slave ship called the *Brookes*. It showed almost five hundred bodies packed tightly on the ship's decks. Versions of the poster were published in London, New York, and Philadelphia, forcing people to face the reality of slavery. It became a powerful tool for groups fighting to abolish the slave trade. It was impossible to look at that diagram and not imagine what it must be like to be one of those people, packed like cargo belowdecks.

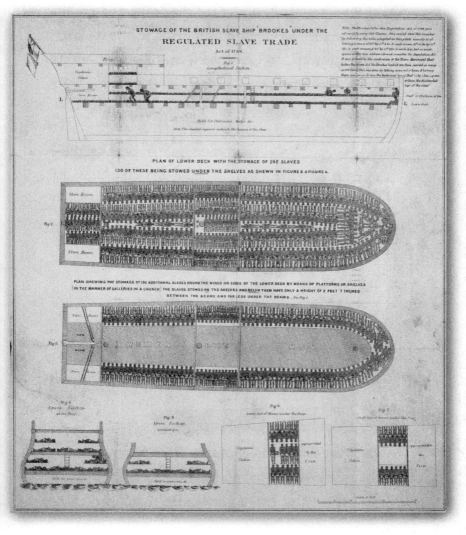

Some people who had profited from transporting enslaved people later fought against slavery. Slave ship captain John Newton had written in his journal about how grateful he was for the "easy and creditable way of life" he enjoyed. But just a few years later, Newton gave up his job to be a minister and wrote that his life had been "unlawful and wrong." He ended up writing the words to a famous hymn.

Amazing grace, how sweet the sound
That saved a wretch like me.
I once was lost, but now am found,
Was blind, but now I see.

But few slave ship captains were willing to give up the money they earned by transporting enslaved people across the sea. Many more continued to be part of the cruel trade. And not just in the American South. Slavery was legal and practiced in all of the thirteen English colonies.

The Dutch, who founded New York (called New Netherland at the time), became the biggest players in the slave trade and brought hundreds of enslaved people to New York in the early days of colonization. When Britain seized New Amsterdam (New York City) in 1664, about a quarter of the people who lived there were enslaved Africans.

New York merchants continued to be heavily involved in the slave trade. They auctioned off enslaved people at a market on Wall Street, where some of the world's biggest banks are today.

A drawing of the slave market of Wall Street
as it looked in the 1700s

Enslaved people were forced to work in homes and shops, on the docks, and on farms on the outskirts of town. This happened all over the northern colonies.

Many more people were enslaved in the South, where they worked on huge plantations. The numbers were staggering. From 1700 to 1780, *twice* as many Africans as Europeans arrived in America. The work of those enslaved people was behind most of the goods exported from the colonies. They truly built America's first economy.

THREE
RESISTANCE AND REVOLTS

By now, you might be wondering when we're going to talk about the Underground Railroad. When do the secret rooms and signal lanterns come into the story? The answer is, not quite yet. Because that traditional idea of the Underground Railroad is really just the tip of the iceberg when it comes to all the ways enslaved people fought back against their captors.

The resistance that had begun in Africa and on the ships that carried people to the Americas continued after they arrived. Most of the enslaved people brought across the Atlantic ended up in the Caribbean islands colonized by the British, working on sugar plantations. Others would land in the English colonies of North America.

A ship full of enslaved African people arrived in the colony of Jamestown in 1619. They'd been seized by a privateer, a sort of government-sanctioned pirate who took them from a Portuguese ship. Those twenty to thirty people were sold to the Jamestown colonists. They were the first of about four hundred thousand enslaved Africans forced into labor in what would become the United States of America.

An illustration of enslaved Africans landing at Jamestown in 1619, by Howard Pyle, 1901

Virginia also had indentured servants, who came to America of their own free will. These people had signed contracts to work for a number of years, often to pay back the cost of their travel to the colony. Almost as soon as Virginia was established, powerful men in the colony began passing laws to control the people forced to work for them. Enslaved people who escaped were treated as lost property to be returned to their enslavers. Virginia's Runaway Servants Act of 1643 called for indentured servants caught trying to run away to serve *twice* as long as the terms in their contracts. If a person ran away a second time, they'd have the letter *R* branded, or burned, onto their cheek.

In spite of those laws, enslaved people continued to fight back against their captors. There were numerous uprisings in the Caribbean in the 1500s. Most were crushed, but some people escaped. The revolts were violent, and even those that failed sent a message to enslavers: if you think you're safe, think again.

The largest uprising of enslaved people in mainland America happened near Charleston, South Carolina, in September 1739. Known as the Stono Rebellion, it began when about twenty enslaved people gathered at the Stono River, determined to fight for their freedom.

They raided a store and then went from house to house, killing white people as they headed south. As they advanced, more enslaved people joined them until the uprising was about a hundred people strong.

The group fought off the English for more than a week, until most of the freedom fighters were killed. But some escaped, possibly to a place called Fort Mose, which had become a haven for enslaved people seeking freedom.

THE STORY OF FORT MOSE

We think of the Underground Railroad as leading north to freedom, but many enslaved people actually escaped by running *south*. In the early days of colonization, England, France, and Spain were all fighting for territory. The land we now call Florida was controlled by Spain, and Spain wanted to keep it. So in 1693, King Charles II invited Africans who were enslaved in the British colonies to escape to Spanish Florida. There, they could live as free men, but the king's order included a few conditions.

Edict of 1693

Enslaved Africans who escape to Spanish Florida must:

- Become Catholic
- Swear allegiance to the king
- Serve four years in the military

Even with some strings attached, the deal must have looked pretty good when compared with enslavement. People started taking the king up on his offer.

The English were horrified. How dare the Spanish encourage enslaved people to sneak away! How would their plantations survive without workers? In the last twenty years, rice production in the English colonies had sky-rocketed. Without the free labor of enslaved people, the English couldn't keep up that pace. They wouldn't be able to sustain their way of life. And worst of all, Spain was going to give those newly freed Black men weapons!

But the English couldn't stop the flood of enslaved people heading south. Native people who lived in the area knew the best and safest routes and helped them along.

By 1738, more than a hundred freedom seekers had arrived, and the Spanish gover-nor of Florida created a settlement for them, called Fort Mose (pronounced MOH-say). It was built just north of St. Augustine to help defend the colony from the English. Men who had escaped from the English plantations defended the fort and built homes nearby for their families.

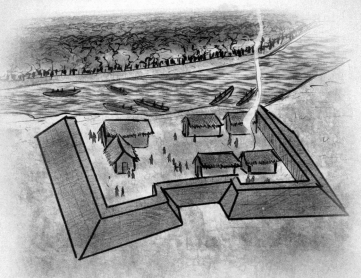

You might think the Spanish were pretty great for helping enslaved people like that. But they weren't antislavery. Slavery was legal in Spanish Florida, so taking in enslaved people from the English colonies wasn't something the Spanish did because they were good guys. They did it because they wanted to make life difficult for the English, and they also wanted more people to defend Spanish land. Those men who had escaped from the English

did a good job protecting their new home.

The leader of the free Black militia at Fort Mose was Captain Francisco Menéndez. When the British attacked the fort in 1740, Menéndez and his men had to flee but later returned to take back their village. They defeated the English in what is now called the Battle of Bloody Mose.

Fort Mose was destroyed in the siege, but the Spanish rebuilt it in a different location in 1752. The Black militia continued to defend that new site until 1763, when Spain gave up Florida to England. Then the Black Spanish community abandoned the fort, and many fled to Cuba.

In the years that followed, the remains of Fort Mose were swallowed up by a marsh and lost to history for a while. Later, a team of archaeologists helped to restore the site, which is now a National Historic Landmark in St. Augustine. Today, Fort Mose is known as the first free African American settlement in America.

While some enslaved people fled to Spanish Florida, others escaped into the wilderness. The Great Dismal Swamp, which covered parts of Virginia and North Carolina, was a popular destination. It was a vast, wild wetland, thick with mud, thorns, and submerged roots, inhabited by bears, venomous snakes, and thick swarms of mosquitoes. No one wanted to go there to track people down, and that made it a perfect hiding place.

In the early 1600s, there were reports of Native people finding refuge in the swamp as they fled from attacking colonists. Black freedom seekers joined them, and by the end of the century, whole communities had sprung up.

People who escaped from slavery and set up their own free settlements were called maroons, a term that likely came from the Spanish word *cimarrón,* which was originally used to refer to escaped livestock. Maroons were individuals from different societies in Africa who had come together to set up a new community that reflected all of their cultures.

Because maroon settlements were by their very nature a secret, there aren't many details about them in the historical record. For a long time, many people didn't believe that maroons were establishing long-term communities. They figured that people who had escaped from slavery hid in the swamp for a while but certainly didn't make permanent homes there.

But historians have found that many did just that. Archaeologists have discovered evidence of cabins, along with the remains of tools, weapons, and white clay pipes. Those artifacts tell the story of people who really did escape from slavery to set up their own free and independent communities. They came up with ways to get the things they needed to survive. There are written accounts of enslaved people raiding farms and escaping into the swamps with livestock. In 1714, Virginia's lieutenant governor called the swamp a no-man's-land, full of "loose and disorderly people." Another man led a survey into the swamp to find the state boundary between Virginia and North Carolina and wrote about finding a whole family of maroons.

"It is certain many Slaves Shelter themselves in this Obscure Part of the World."

—WILLIAM BYRD II, 1728

When people escaped from slavery, their enslavers often posted notices in newspapers to try to get them back. Many of these ads mentioned the Great Dismal Swamp as a possible destination.

The people who fled there cleared fields and built homes on areas of higher ground. They grew corn and trapped hogs and wild birds. People tended gardens, hunted, and caught fish while their children played together. Similar communities sprang up outside New Orleans, in Alabama, and in Florida. The locations weren't ideal, and it wasn't an easy life, but the people there were free. That mattered more than anything else.

FOUR
LIBERTY FOR SOME

You've probably heard stories about the American Revolution, when American colonists went to war to be free of British rule. The war disrupted everyday life in the colonies. Men left their farms and homes to fight on both sides of the conflict. Patriots who supported breaking away from Great Britain talked a lot about freedom, but that freedom was never meant to extend to those who were enslaved. Still, the chaos of the war offered enslaved people new opportunities to escape.

Before it was over, both sides in the Revolutionary War—the Americans and the British, or

Redcoats—used enslaved people to fight their battles for them. And both made promises about freedom that weren't always kept.

IN 1775, LORD DUNMORE, THE ROYAL GOVERNOR OF VIRGINIA, OFFERED FREEDOM TO ENSLAVED PEOPLE WHO ESCAPED FROM PATRIOTS AND ENLISTED IN THE BRITISH ARMY.

THIS GROUP OF SOLDIERS, CALLED LORD DUNMORE'S ETHIOPIAN REGIMENT, WORE UNIFORMS EMBROIDERED WITH THE PROMISE THE BRITISH HAD MADE.

TENS OF THOUSANDS OF ENSLAVED PEOPLE MAY HAVE TRIED TO JOIN THE BRITISH, HOPING FOR FREEDOM.

FOR MOST, IT DIDN'T WORK OUT. SOME NEVER MADE IT TO THE BRITISH . . .

. . . AND MANY OF THOSE WHO DID ENDED UP DYING OF SMALLPOX.

WHEN GEORGE WASHINGTON FIRST TOOK COMMAND OF THE CONTINENTAL ARMY, HE WOULDN'T LET ENSLAVED PEOPLE ENLIST AT ALL. LATER, HE WAS FORCED TO CHANGE THAT POLICY BECAUSE HE DIDN'T HAVE ENOUGH MEN.

AT THE TIME OF THE WAR, WASHINGTON ENSLAVED MORE THAN A HUNDRED PEOPLE ON HIS MOUNT VERNON PLANTATION IN VIRGINIA.

SOME ENDED UP ESCAPING TO JOIN THE BRITISH.

AN ENSLAVED MAN NAMED HARRY HAD TRIED TO ESCAPE FROM MOUNT VERNON IN 1771 BUT WAS CAUGHT AND RETURNED.

IN 1776, HARRY FLED AGAIN, JOINING THE REDCOATS, AND EVENTUALLY BECAME A CORPORAL IN THE BRITISH ARMY.

WHEN THE WAR ENDED, THE BRITISH SENT SOME OF THE ENSLAVED PEOPLE WHO'D SERVED WITH THEM ON A SHIP TO NOVA SCOTIA, WHERE THEY COULD LIVE IN A FREE SETTLEMENT. THAT'S WHERE HARRY WENT AFTER THE WAR.

BUT MANY OTHERS WHO ESCAPED FROM SLAVERY TO SERVE THE BRITISH FOUND THEMSELVES BACK IN CHAINS.

After the war, enslavers went hunting for the people who had escaped from them. George Washington sent men out to track down the people he'd enslaved. He found two of them near Yorktown and several more in Philadelphia. Washington returned them to slavery for the rest of their lives.

You might think that once the United States was a free nation, it would do something about the injustice of slavery. After all, it would be pretty hypocritical to fight an entire war about liberty, only to keep enslaving people, right? But that's exactly what the new nation did. America's founding documents had little to say about slavery.

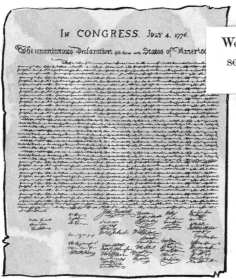

We hold these truths to be self-evident, that all men are created equal.

That line in the Declaration of Independence sounds nice, but it didn't include enslaved people. An early draft of the declaration did have a line about how slavery was a cruel practice, but that got edited out before the final version was approved.

The US Constitution, the framework for America's government, didn't abolish slavery, either. But it also didn't promise that slavery would be around forever. The Constitution doesn't use the words "slavery" and "slave" at all, but it does address the issue.

ARTICLE I, SECTION 9, CLAUSE 1, OF THE US CONSTITUTION
The Migration or Importation of such Persons as any of the States now existing shall think proper to admit, shall not be prohibited by the Congress prior to the Year one thousand eight hundred and eight, but a Tax or duty may be imposed on such Importation, not exceeding ten dollars for each Person.

In other words: Congress won't pass laws banning slavery until at least 1808. But it might tax enslavers.

That clause was controversial. Southern lawmakers complained that even *suggesting* slavery might go away someday was just the North trying to deprive southern property owners of their rights. Some northern lawmakers thought it was awful that a nation would establish its own independence only to enslave others. But Roger Sherman, who signed both the Declaration of Independence and the Constitution, said fighting over slavery wasn't worth splitting up the new country.

The Constitution also included rules to help out enslavers.

ARTICLE IV, SECTION 2, CLAUSE 3, OF THE US CONSTITUTION
No Person held to Service or Labour in one State, under the Laws thereof, escaping into another, shall, in Consequence of any Law or Regulation therein, be discharged from such Service or Labour, but shall be delivered up on Claim of the Party to whom such Service or Labour may be due.

In other words: If an enslaved person escapes to another state, that doesn't mean they're free. They'll just be returned to their enslavers.

Another part of the Constitution, known as the three-fifths clause, explains that people who weren't free literally didn't count as much as everyone else in the new nation. This clause set up a system where each enslaved individual would count for three-fifths of a person when populations were added up for the purpose of determining how many representatives a state would get in Congress.

Even though the writers of the Declaration of Independence and the Constitution never meant to promise freedom for enslaved people, their words inspired some to seek freedom on their own.

An enslaved woman named Mumbet went to court to fight for her freedom in Massachusetts in 1781. She's believed to have been inspired by either the Declaration of Independence or the Massachusetts Constitution, which uses similar language about equality.

Mumbet won her freedom and renamed herself Elizabeth Freeman. Two years later, the Supreme Court of Massachusetts ruled that slavery was abolished under the state's constitution. Others continued to seek freedom as well, whether they were enslaved by simple farmers or by the president of the United States.

FREEDOM FOR ONA JUDGE

Ona Judge was born enslaved on George Washington's plantation. Her mother taught her how to sew, and that kept her out of the fields, where long hours and brutal working conditions often led to early deaths. When Washington became president, Judge went with him and his wife, Martha, to New York and then Philadelphia.

That move changed her life. Now Judge wore pretty clothes as she accompanied the First Lady throughout the city. She also met free Black people and began to plan a new future for herself. She would run away and live her life as a free person!

The free Black people Judge had met helped her plan her escape. On the assigned day, she boarded a ship called the *Nancy* and sailed north to Portsmouth, New Hampshire. There, other free Black people found her a place to live, and she got a job working as a maid.

May 24, 1796—The Washingtons placed this ad in the *Pennsylvania Gazette*, offering a reward for Ona Judge's return to enslavement.

But Judge's happiness didn't last. One day, a friend of the Washingtons recognized her. The president sent a local official named Joseph Whipple to find her and convince her to return to the Washingtons. Ona Judge said she'd go back—but only if George and Martha promised to free her after their deaths.

George Washington was furious. He knew the law allowed him to capture Ona Judge by force, but he also understood that it would be a pretty bad look for the president to violently seize a woman from a northern state where many people were against slavery. He kept trying to recapture her without attracting too much attention but was never successful. Ona Judge married a free Black sailor, had three children, and lived the rest of her life in freedom.

Because the US Constitution didn't include specific laws about slavery, each state got to decide for itself. Vermont abolished slavery in its constitution in 1777, before the Revolutionary War had even ended, and was admitted to the union in 1791 with a total ban on slavery. By 1804, all the other northern states had voted to follow.

But they didn't prohibit all slavery overnight. Instead, many laws called for "gradual abolition." Sometimes that meant setting a future date for the end of slavery. Enslaved people were freed after they reached a certain age or finished working for a certain number of years.

Once those changes took effect, more people who escaped from slavery in the South began making their way to northern states, where some people might offer help and the laws offered at least a little bit of protection. Enslavers didn't like that, and they fought back.

A LAW TO HELP ENSLAVERS

In 1791, the states of Virginia and Pennsylvania got in a fight over a man named John

Davis. Davis was an enslaved man who'd been freed by Pennsylvania's Gradual Abolition Act, one of those state laws to get rid of slavery little by little. Three Virginia men who insisted that Davis was still someone's "property" showed up in Pennsylvania, kidnapped him, and took him to Virginia.

Pennsylvania's governor demanded that those three men be returned to his state to be charged with kidnapping. Virginia's governor said no. So the governor of Pennsylvania asked President George Washington to step in. He wanted the president to have Congress make it clear how people who were accused of escaping from slavery could and could not be recovered. Did they really want men running around kidnapping people?

You might think this is the part of the story where the US Congress steps in to protect freedom seekers. But that's not what happened. Instead, Congress passed the Fugitive Slave Act of 1793, which said enslavers were free to track down anyone who ran away.

The law said an enslaver was allowed to seize an accused runaway and bring them before a judge with any sort of evidence. That "proof" could be as flimsy as a white man pointing and saying, "Hey, that's my slave."

Then the judge would issue something called a "certificate of removal," allowing the person to be taken back into slavery. Anyone who tried to interfere could be sued. The law didn't give enslaved people the right to a fair trial or even a chance to speak up for themselves.

The Fugitive Slave Act wasn't the only bad news for enslaved people in 1793. That was also the year that Eli Whitney invented the cotton gin.

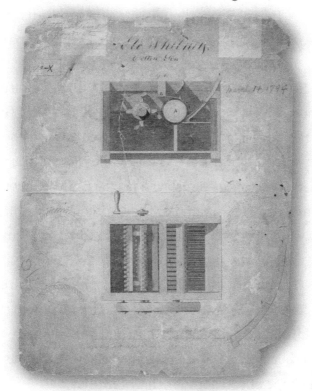

Eli Whitney's original patent for the cotton gin

This machine separated cotton seeds from fibers and made it faster to produce cotton. It was an opportunity to make money, so the United States forced Cherokee, Chickasaw, Choctaw, Creek, and Seminole people from their land to clear the way for white settlers to grow more cotton. And then, of course, cotton producers needed more enslaved people to work in the fields. Even though many Americans knew slavery was wrong, it became an even bigger part of the new country's economy.

But at the same time, little by little, attitudes about slavery were changing. In 1807, both Great Britain and the United States passed laws to abolish the international slave trade. That was supposed to mean that no more enslaved people could be brought from Africa to England or the United States. But the law wasn't enforced all that well, and it only banned the slave *trade*—not slavery itself.

That didn't help the millions of people already enslaved in the United States. And it didn't help their children, who were enslaved from the moment they were born. More and more people saw escape as the only hope of freedom for their families.

FIVE
FREEDOM'S FIRE

As ideas about liberty continued to spread after the American Revolution, more and more enslaved people decided that if the law wouldn't give them freedom, they'd take it. Sometimes that meant escaping from slavery, and sometimes it meant fighting their enslavers.

Not long after America declared independence from Great Britain, enslaved people on the Caribbean island of Saint-Domingue staged their own revolution. They rose up against their French enslavers, killed white people, and burned plantations. This led to the abolition of slavery on Saint-Domingue in

1793. The French sent troops to the island, hoping to restore colonial rule and bring back slavery. But many of those soldiers died of yellow fever, which was widespread there. Those French forces ended up getting crushed by disease and by an army of people who used to be enslaved.

A man named Toussaint Louverture led the Black troops. The son of an educated enslaved man, Toussaint was a powerful military leader who trained his followers and used his knowledge of the island to outsmart the French. His troops were victorious, and the former colony declared its independence as Haiti—the first Black republic in the world.

INDEPENDENCE DEBT

After the revolution, French enslavers wanted payment for the people they claimed were lost "property." France demanded that Haiti pay $150 million (later reduced to $90 million) or face another war, even though they'd already fought for and won their independence. It would take the new republic more than a hundred years to pay that crippling debt.

News of that successful revolt scared other white enslavers. What if the people they enslaved rose up against them, too? They had good reason to worry. The story of the Haitian Revolution inspired other enslaved people and led to uprisings in the English colonies as well.

IN VIRGINIA IN 1799, GABRIEL PROSSER AND TWO OTHER ENSLAVED MEN WERE ACCUSED OF STEALING A PIG.

WHEN THE WHITE OVERSEER CAUGHT THEM, PROSSER WRESTLED THE MAN TO THE GROUND AND BIT OFF MOST OF HIS EAR.

PROSSER RECEIVED A HARSH PUNISHMENT THAT MADE HIM DETERMINED TO FIGHT BACK.

HE MADE A PLAN TO SEIZE CAPITOL SQUARE IN RICHMOND AND TAKE THE GOVERNOR HOSTAGE! HE BELIEVED THAT IF ENSLAVED PEOPLE ROSE UP, POOR WHITE PEOPLE WOULD JOIN THEM, SO HE STARTED RECRUITING.

PROSSER WAS AN EXCELLENT BLACKSMITH. HE MADE SWORDS OUT OF FARM EQUIPMENT TO PREPARE FOR THE UPRISING. THE RAID WAS PLANNED FOR AUGUST 30, 1800.

BUT THAT DAY, RAIN POURED DOWN IN BUCKETS.

THE ROADS AND BRIDGES WERE IMPASSABLE, SO PROSSER POSTPONED THE REVOLT.

BUT BY THEN SOME MEN HAD GROWN NERVOUS AND TOLD THEIR ENSLAVERS ABOUT THE PLAN.

ABOUT THIRTY PEOPLE WHO'D BEEN PART OF THE PLOT WERE ARRESTED.

PROSSER ESCAPED. HE SWAM OUT TO A SCHOONER ON THE JAMES RIVER AND CONVINCED THE CAPTAIN TO HELP HIM.

BUT ANOTHER MAN RATTED PROSSER OUT! WHEN THE SHIP LANDED, AUTHORITIES WERE WAITING. THEY ARRESTED PROSSER, PUT HIM ON TRIAL, AND SENTENCED HIM TO DEATH, ALONG WITH MORE THAN TWO DOZEN OTHER PEOPLE WHO HAD TRIED TO FIGHT FOR THEIR FREEDOM.

This was how uprisings typically ended. People who organized resistance knew the risks and understood that the odds were against them. But anything was better than the inhumanity of slavery. And once ideas about freedom caught fire, the flames were hard to put out.

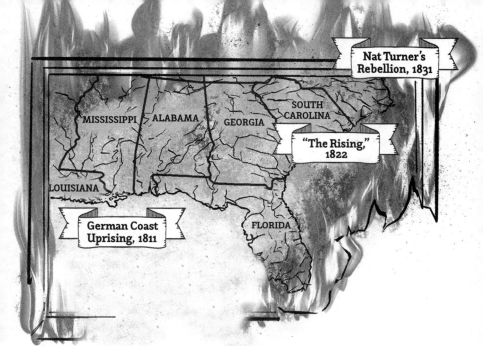

In 1811, Charles Deslondes planned and led what is now called the German Coast uprising, in Louisiana. His army was made up of hundreds of enslaved people who risked everything to fight for their freedom. They marched toward New Orleans, burning plantations. Eventually, the local militia caught up with them, killing dozens and taking many more prisoner before the rest fled to the swamps. In the end, a hundred people were executed for taking part in that rebellion.

Denmark Vesey was inspired by stories out of Haiti to lead his own revolt in Charleston, South

Carolina, in 1822. Vesey held meetings and collected weapons, hoping that as many as nine thousand enslaved people would join him in the revolt now known as "the rising" and they could all escape to Haiti. But once again, someone betrayed the plan. Vesey was arrested and executed along with about thirty-five other people. Another thirty-five were sold to plantations in the West Indies. If Vesey's uprising hadn't been stopped, it would have been the largest revolt of enslaved people in US history.

Denmark Vesey's legacy is honored with a monument at Hampton Park in Charleston, South Carolina.

Perhaps the most famous rebellion of enslaved people was led by a man named Nat Turner. Enslaved in Virginia, he was deeply religious and believed God had called him to free people.

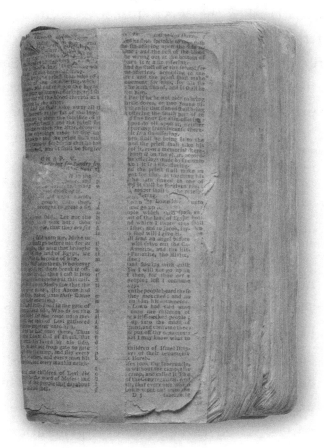

Nat Turner's Bible is on display at the Smithsonian's National Museum of African American History and Culture.

One August night in 1831, Turner and his followers killed their enslaver and his family. Then they marched through Southampton County, Virginia, and killed dozens of other white people before the state militia crushed the revolt. Turner escaped but was later captured and executed, along with more than fifty others. After the rebellion, white mobs in South Carolina murdered nearly two hundred Black people, many of whom had nothing to do with the revolt.

NAT TURNER'S SKULL

After Nat Turner's death, there was a lot of mystery over what happened to his remains. The doctor who handled Turner's body after his execution reportedly kept his skull. The doctor eventually handed it down to his own daughter. She gave it to a Virginia doctor, who passed it on to his kids. The unusual inheritance passed through several generations, always kept in a box with a note about whose skull it was.

Next, it was given to civil rights activists, who donated it to the mayor of Gary, Indiana, for a Civil Rights Hall of Fame project. The mayor hung on to it until he was contacted by Turner's descendants, and then he turned the skull over to them. It was sent to the Smithsonian Institution for analysis to determine if it really is Turner's remains.

Nat Turner descendant Shanna Batten Aguirre said that the skull is "a poignant reminder of the price of freedom. In a very tangible way, it asserts the humanity of people who were systemically dehumanized. Its incredible existence demands acknowledgment that, yes, this Black life mattered."

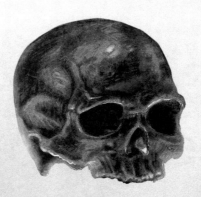

Not all revolts of enslaved people ended in tragedy. In 1841, a ship called the *Creole* was bringing more than a hundred enslaved people to New Orleans to be sold. An enslaved man named Madison Washington and seventeen others overpowered the ship's crew. They gathered all the weapons and the documents related to their enslavement and forced one of the crew members to take them to the Bahamas, which was then a British colony. Slavery was illegal there, so when they arrived, they were free. The British did arrest the people who'd planned the revolt, but they were eventually released. One hundred twenty-eight people sailed to freedom in that uprising—the most successful revolt of enslaved people in US history.

While some enslaved people claimed their freedom through uprisings, others planned quieter escapes. Once northern states began passing laws to get rid of slavery, more enslaved people dared to run away. Now they could set out for safe—or at least *safer*—destinations instead of simply hiding out in swamps or hoping to disappear into busy cities.

Sometimes, people escaping from slavery got various kinds of help, including shelter. This is what most people think of when they hear the term "Underground Railroad"—a secret network of hiding places, run by antislavery "conductors" who hurried freedom seekers along from one safe house to the next as they traveled north. But is this a story that needs a little smashing?

The truth is, that world of hidden rooms and secret helpers *did* exist. However, it was just one small part of the overall picture when it came to enslaved people claiming their freedom.

Enslaved people in Maryland, Virginia, and Kentucky could sometimes escape into bordering states to the north, where there were laws against slavery and large populations of free Black people to offer help. But that was much harder for people enslaved in the Deep South, who would have had to pass through many more miles of slave states before they found safety.

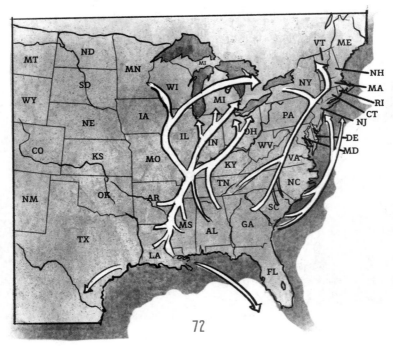

Northern states weren't the only places where slavery was illegal. After Mexico abolished slavery in 1829, a network of Mexican Americans and biracial couples along the border helped enslaved people make their way through Texas to Mexico. Historians have uncovered stories about at least two family ranches along the Rio Grande that are believed to have been stops on this southern Underground Railroad.

Ads placed in Texas newspapers show that enslavers knew about this southern route to freedom and tried to recover the people who fled there.

But Mexico wasn't a safe place for slave catchers. Sometimes they'd arrive to find armed villagers protecting the freedom seekers. Instead of being recaptured, many of those who escaped took Spanish names, raised families, and moved farther into Mexico.

In other parts of the South, enslaved people escaped by ship to British islands like the Bahamas, where slavery had been abolished. Others found refuge with Florida's Native people, who had also suffered brutal treatment at the hands of European colonists. More than twenty-five thousand Chickasaw, Choctaw, and Creek people lived in the areas around Pensacola, Florida. They'd fought against the British and welcomed enslaved people who fled to their lands.

Seminole people also helped enslaved people in Florida. Although they practiced racial slavery, the Seminole sometimes welcomed Black people who'd escaped from slavery as full members of their tribe. Descendants of these Black Seminole people still live in Oklahoma, Florida, Texas, the Bahamas, and northern Mexico.

WHILE MANY FREE BLACK PEOPLE LIVED IN FLORIDA, OTHERS WERE ENSLAVED THERE. SOME WERE HIRED OUT TO WORK AT THE PENSACOLA NAVY YARD.

ONE OF THEM WAS AN ENSLAVED BLACKSMITH NAMED ADAM.

IN 1850, HE DECIDED IT WAS TIME TO ESCAPE.

HE STOWED AWAY ON A SHIP CALLED THE MARY FARROW.

FOR THREE DAYS, HE HID IN THE SHIP'S HOLD . . .

. . . UNTIL THE CAPTAIN DISCOVERED HIS HIDING PLACE.

Once enslaved men like Adam reached a northern state, abolitionists sometimes offered help in the form of shelter, transportation, or legal assistance.

But most enslaved people had to escape on their own. Many failed. Those who succeeded did so with ingenuity, determination, and courage. The role of white helpers was often overplayed in history books, while Black abolitionists who took the greatest risks were forgotten.

SIX
HEROES AND HELPERS

I f you've heard stories about the Underground Railroad, there's a good chance that the heroes of those tales were Quakers, those "good white people" who helped enslaved people escape. The Quakers were a Christian religious group that first came to America in the late 1600s. The story of an entire religion fighting slavery is part myth and part true. We'll talk about the true part first.

Many Quakers *were* antislavery, and some *did* help freedom seekers. Even in the early days of the colonies, some Quakers spoke up against slavery, saying it was unchristian.

In 1754, Philadelphia Quakers made it official by publishing an open letter against slavery, and by the 1770s, being antislavery was a big part of the Quaker belief system. Quakers looked at slavery as a "national evil." Some argued that they should actively work to fight it, even if that meant breaking laws. The government might have said slavery was fine, but the Quakers were pretty sure God would disagree, and they were going with God on this one. It wasn't a popular view at the time.

Even before he became president, George Washington was aware that Quakers and others were working to help freedom seekers. Washington said

he looked forward to seeing slavery abolished—
someday—but he also said that while it was still legal,
people ought to respect the law. In one letter, Washington even suggested that some people were *happier*
being enslaved.

"But when slaves who are happy & content to remain with their present masters, are tampered with & seduced to leave them; when masters are taken at unawares by these practices; when a conduct of this sort begets discontent on one side and resentment on the other, & when it happens to fall on a man whose purse will not measure with that of the Society, & he looses his property for want of means to defend it—it is oppression in the latter case, & not humanity in any; because it introduces more evils than it can cure."

—GEORGE WASHINGTON'S
LETTER TO ROBERT MORRIS,
APRIL 12, 1786

In other words: Sometimes people are perfectly
happy being enslaved, and when abolitionists convince them to escape, everybody gets upset and it
creates more problems than it's worth.

As you can imagine, people who were enslaved felt differently about this. So did many Quakers. But some thought that abolition—getting rid of slavery entirely—was too extreme and would lead to violence, which their religion also had a problem with. Quakers were against war, so if opposing slavery led to a war, well, that was kind of a mess.

Quakers who did actively fight slavery faced pushback. Many northern merchants earned a lot of money selling goods produced by enslaved people. Other people thought slavery was wrong but looked the other way and didn't appreciate their antislavery neighbors causing trouble.

After the Union won the American Civil War, being against slavery was suddenly more popular. People who had been antislavery all along wanted everybody to know about it. That's when a number of Quakers and other white abolitionists published memoirs and recollections of their work. Sometimes those stories were exaggerated to make them more exciting, and this is the source of some of the myths surrounding the Underground Railroad. Most people escaping from slavery probably stayed in attics or barns, but hidden rooms with secret passages are more fun to talk about, so those stories got told—and shared. And many Quaker writers of these stories, like M. B. Butler, seemed determined to get credit for being good guys.

> "Considering the kind of labor performed, the expense incurred and the danger involved, one must be impressed with the unselfish devotion to principle, of these men and women thus engaged. There was for them no outward honor, no material recompense."
> —M. B. BUTLER, *MY STORY OF THE CIVIL WAR AND THE UNDERGROUND RAILROAD*

In other words: You should be impressed with me! We didn't get much credit for being so awesome and brave at the time, and I'd like that credit now, please.

Another Quaker, named Levi Coffin, helped people escaping from slavery when they arrived in

Indiana, where he lived. Coffin is believed to have helped hundreds of freedom seekers, but like Butler, he wasn't exactly humble about it when he wrote the story of his life.

Friends in the neighborhood, who had formerly stood aloof from the work, fearful of the penalty of the law, were encouraged to engage in it when they saw the fearless manner in which I acted, and the success that attended my efforts.

In other words: People were afraid to help out, but they stepped up when they saw how awesome and brave I was.

Coffin also criticized the many Black people in his area who helped people escape from slavery, claiming that the enslaved people they helped were often captured because the Black helpers weren't good at hiding them and sneaking them into Canada. What Coffin didn't mention—or maybe didn't notice—was that it was more likely his own privilege as a white man that made his work easier. Black people who worked with the Underground Railroad would have been subject to far more scrutiny and faced harsher penalties if they were caught.

A PLACE FOR EVERYONE

Bragging aside, some Quaker families really did make it their life mission to take action against slavery. Rowland and Rachel Robinson were Vermont Quakers who refused to buy anything made by enslaved people. They ran a sheep farm called Rokeby, where they hired freedom seekers making their way north.

The Robinsons offered paid work and a place to stay for people escaping from slavery. You might be picturing one of those secret, hidden rooms from Underground Railroad legends, but at Rokeby, freedom seekers who were passing through slept in a regular bedroom, with a window that looked out onto the road.

An upstairs bedroom at the Robinson farm

The Robinsons weren't shy about helping enslaved people. They didn't need to be. Vermont was full of antislavery activists, and the Robinsons were a fairly powerful family, so even people who disagreed with them tended to be pretty quiet about it. The Robinsons even ran an interracial school on their farm; anyone who wanted to learn was welcome.

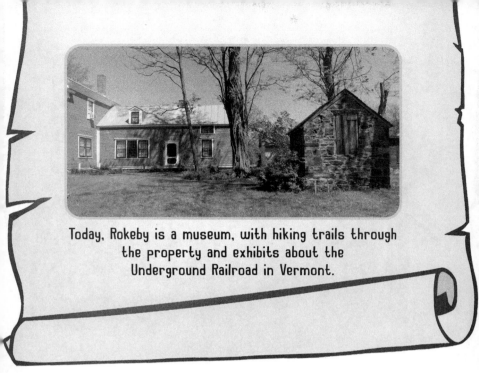

Today, Rokeby is a museum, with hiking trails through the property and exhibits about the Underground Railroad in Vermont.

Most freedom seekers who got help along the way were assisted by other Black people. Free Blacks and those who had already escaped from slavery were the beating heart of the Underground Railroad. They lived mostly in cities and helped hundreds of freedom seekers each year. Many of those new arrivals joined the fight, too.

So, what kinds of help could people hope for when the time came to escape?

Sometimes Black sailors would help people sneak onto ships leaving southern ports.

Black seamen also provided important information to enslaved people, including news about laws and opinions in the North and details about the coast and which captains might be willing to help. They carried letters between enslaved people and their friends and relatives in the North. In fact, Black sailors and dockworkers played such a big role in the Underground Railroad that a white letter writer to North Carolina's *Wilmington Journal* argued that only white men should be hired to do those jobs so enslaved people would stop getting so much help.

Once freedom seekers arrived in the North, abolitionists might give them money, food, or a place to stay. Those with legal knowledge would defend them in court. Others provided money for train tickets or sewed clothes for people so they wouldn't appear to be enslaved when they traveled. People in all walks of life helped in the fight for freedom, using whatever talents and resources they had.

Frances Ellen Watkins Harper had a gift for words. She gave talks and wrote letters against slavery.

Mary Myers hid freedom seekers in her Philadelphia cake shop.

Henrietta Bowers Duterte was Philadelphia's first Black undertaker and worked in a funeral home. She was known to hide freedom seekers in caskets!

While many people fought secret battles against slavery on their own, others organized in local groups. One of those was the Vigilant Association of Philadelphia, which helped people escaping from slavery as they passed through the city. Robert Purvis formed the group in 1837. He was from South Carolina, the son of a wealthy cotton merchant and a free woman of color.

Purvis was also a member of the Pennsylvania Abolition Society. Believe it or not, that group didn't have a single Black member until Purvis joined in 1842. And he was the only one for more than twenty years! Even white people who were against slavery weren't great about including Black people in the conversations about it. But Purvis served as president of the group for five years.

Philadelphia also had a Female Vigilant Association. Elizabeth White was president of this group of fifteen Black women who focused on raising money to help freedom seekers. They'd noticed that while white activists wanted to get rid of slavery, they weren't always interested in helping the real people who escaped and showed up in need. So that's where the Black women focused their efforts. They held public meetings and an annual December fair to raise money.

Black churches also took a leading role in the abolition movement and the Underground Railroad. One of these was the First African Baptist Church of Savannah, Georgia, which still exists.

First African Baptist Church in Savannah, Georgia, is among the oldest Black churches in the United States.

The church was founded by an enslaved man named George Liele. He'd become a Christian by going to church with his enslaver. Liele later became a preacher because he wanted other enslaved people to know God. When the church opened in 1773, it was called the First Colored Baptist Church. It later moved and changed its name.

Was it a stop on the Underground Railroad? Sometimes a house, person, or church is reported to have been part of that secret network, but there may not be written documents to confirm it. Instead, stories are passed down from one family member to another, or from friend to friend. That's the case with this Savannah church. Church historians point to a nine-patch quilt pattern in the ceiling, which was said to mark the church as a safe haven for freedom seekers. They say a second wooden floor built under the regular auditorium floor created space for people escaping from slavery.

Mother Bethel African Methodist Episcopal Church in Philadelphia was also known to help freedom seekers. Founded by Richard Allen, it even had its own publishing house and newspaper.

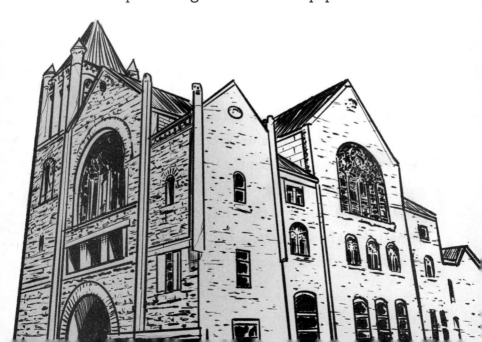

In 1817, Philadelphia's Black leaders held a meeting at Mother Bethel AME Church to talk about a possible solution to slavery. What if enslaved people could be freed and taken back to Africa, where they could have their own colony? Some thought it was a good idea, because they didn't believe Black people would ever be treated fairly in the United States. Others argued that people freed from slavery should stay and demand their rights as US citizens.

The plan to create a colony in Africa also had support from some white people. Racist Americans saw it a way to get rid of Black people living in the country. Some argued that they'd be happier in Africa, where there wasn't so much racism. Right now, you're probably thinking, "Wait a minute. . . . Some people thought it was better to ship people across an ocean instead of dealing with their own racism?" The answer is pretty much yes. That's what they thought.

Supporters of this idea formed a group called the American Colonization Society (ACS) and, in 1822, established a colony for free African Americans on the west coast of Africa.

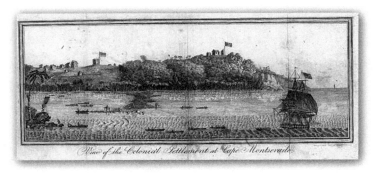

An 1825 drawing, *Home of the Colonial Settlement at Cape Montserado*

In 1847, that colony became the independent nation of Liberia. By 1867, the ACS had sent more than thirteen thousand Black Americans to settle there.

Those who opposed the idea of a return to Africa doubled down on their efforts to make the United States work for everyone. They called for freedom, equal rights, and citizenship for those who were enslaved. The movement to abolish slavery gained more support, and new leaders emerged in the fight for freedom.

Maria Stewart was the first African American woman to publish a political manifesto, or statement of beliefs. She said she'd rather die than be sent away to a colony overseas, and she urged Black people to fight against slavery.

"Many think, because your skins are tinged with a sable hue, that you are an inferior race of beings; but God does not consider you as such. He hath formed and fashioned you in his own glorious image, and hath bestowed upon you reason and strong powers of intellect . . . And according to the Constitution of these United States, he hath made all men free and equal."

—MARIA STEWART, "RELIGION AND THE PURE PRINCIPLES OF MORALITY," 1831

Stewart called on Black men to step forward in the fight for equality. One of those who did was Frederick Douglass.

Formerly enslaved in Maryland, Douglass taught himself to read and escaped. In 1841, he joined the abolitionist movement. He's famous for the autobiography he published four years later. When Douglass was living in Rochester, New York, he provided shelter for freedom seekers on their way to Canada. At one point, he was hiding eleven people in his house!

Douglass wasn't always popular with white anti-slavery activists. Some of them actually warned him that he sounded too smart. They told him white people would like him more if he'd quit sounding so articulate in public. Douglass shut down that idea pretty fast. He continued to speak his mind and founded the antislavery newspaper the *North Star*.

FOLLOWING THE NORTH STAR

The name of Douglass's newspaper comes from a well-known story about the Underground Railroad—the idea that freedom seekers found their way at night by following the North Star. There's even a famous song about this, called "Follow the Drinking Gourd," a reference to the constellation called the Big Dipper, which points to the North Star.

Some people say that song was sung by enslaved people as they escaped and was even used to share coded information, but that myth needs a little smashing.

It is true that some freedom seekers used stars in the night sky, including the North Star, to find their way. And they did sometimes sing spirituals. But the story about "Follow the Drinking Gourd" being full of secret codes is a myth. That particular song wasn't even written until the 1920s.

Publications like the *North Star* helped build the abolitionist movement. In 1942, Stephen and Harriet Myers, who lived in Albany, New York, began to work together on a newspaper called the *Northern Star and Freemen's Advocate.*

When freedom seekers passed through Albany, Harriet would interview them to see what they needed, whether that was clothing or money for a train ticket. Then she'd rally her community to help.

Philadelphia businessman James Forten also helped spread the word about efforts to fight slavery. He gave money to support the *Liberator,* an abolitionist newspaper started by William Lloyd Garrison.

James Forten

Boston abolitionist David Walker published a pamphlet called *Appeal to the Colored Citizens of the World,* encouraging people to rise up against slavery. The booklet was sometimes sewn into the linings of sailors' uniforms so free Black sailors could hand it out in secret when they traveled through the South.

It was truly dangerous for free Black people to help others escape from slavery. White people who helped out sometimes had to pay fines when they were sued by enslavers, but punishments were much more severe for Black people. A Black sailor named William Brodie was fined by a Georgia court for helping enslaved people escape. He ended up being sold into slavery himself when he didn't have enough money to pay the fine. When Black abolitionist Charles Torrey was convicted of helping some enslaved people escape, he spent the rest of his life in prison. Despite the risks, Black activists continued to fight slavery with both words and actions.

Some stories about the Underground Railroad make it seem like an official and well-known system that everyone knew about—as if an enslaved person could flee from a plantation and ask around for directions. But that's another myth worth smashing.

Some enslaved people were aware that there might be help out there, but there was no guidebook. They didn't ask about the "Underground Railroad," because that phrase didn't even exist in the early 1800s. Nobody's sure when people started using it, but it didn't show up in historical documents until 1839, when a newspaper quoted an enslaved man who said he hoped to escape on a railroad that "went underground all the way to Boston." The idea seems to have caught on: a few years later, a newspaper in Albany, New York, reported that some fugitives had come through the city via the Underground Railroad. By the 1850s, the phrase was commonly used to describe help given to freedom seekers.

No matter how many stories are told about the Underground Railroad, historical documents show that most freedom seekers had to escape on their own. Usually, if enslaved people got help, it was once they arrived in the North, after the hardest part of their journey was over. To make it that far, they had to be brave, brilliant, and determined to find freedom no matter what.

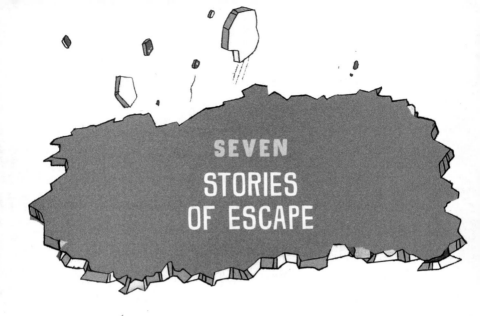

SEVEN

STORIES OF ESCAPE

Many stories from the Underground Railroad are lost to history because they were never recorded. There was good reason for that; keeping records could put both enslaved people and those who assisted them at risk. But one Black abolitionist who helped hundreds of people escape from slavery dared to write it all down.

William Still was born in New Jersey in 1821. His father had been enslaved

but bought his freedom, and his mother had escaped from her enslavers with two of the four children she had at the time. In 1847, the Pennsylvania Anti-Slavery Society hired Still to serve as a clerk and janitor. That's what the official records said, anyway. But Still ended up pretty much running the group. He helped more than four hundred people escape from slavery and kept extensive records. He wrote down their stories but was careful not to share their real names as he recorded the details of their daring escapes. In 1872, Still published an account of the people he had helped as they passed through Philadelphia.

The stories in William Still's book focus not on his work but on the freedom seekers themselves. They also provide real-deal details that contradict some of the myths surrounding the Underground Railroad. For example, history books often show illustrations of a single enslaved person running through the woods. While that did happen sometimes, it wasn't the whole story, so the idea that people always escaped from slavery alone and on foot needs a little smashing.

By the 1850s, many people who escaped from

slavery fled in groups and had some sort of transportation. Many escaped on ships. Still wrote about a man he called Captain F, a burly, scary-looking guy who often helped enslaved people escape in his schooner as he sailed north from Virginia. That captain, whose full name was Albert Fountain, hid enslaved people in the hold of his ship with the wheat.

One day, the Norfolk mayor heard a rumor that Fountain was helping people escape, so he showed up at the dock with a bunch of officers carrying axes and spears. The captain was hiding enslaved people under the deck but knew they'd be discovered if he tried to resist, so he told the officers to go ahead and search. They started spearing the wheat and then set to work on the deck with their axes. When Captain Fountain grew tired of watching them hack at his boat, he grabbed an ax and started going at it himself.

The captain was a big guy, and splinters flew everywhere. The mayor and his officers decided they'd had enough, so they left, and the captain took off for Philadelphia with his hidden freedom seekers still safe and sound belowdecks.

One of the most famous stories William Still recorded was the escape of a man who came to be known as Henry "Box" Brown. His nickname came from his method of escape.

HENRY BROWN WAS ENSLAVED IN VIRGINIA AND HAD BEEN HIRED OUT TO WORK IN A TOBACCO FACTORY.

HE LONGED FOR FREEDOM AND PRAYED FOR GOD'S HELP.

". . . WHEN THE IDEA SUDDENLY FLASHED ACROSS MY MIND OF SHUTTING MYSELF UP IN A BOX, AND GETTING MYSELF CONVEYED AS DRY GOODS TO A FREE STATE."

BROWN'S FRIEND JAMES CAESAR ANTHONY SMITH AND A WHITE MAN NAMED SAMUEL SMITH HELPED WITH HIS PLAN. ON MARCH 29, 1849, BROWN CLIMBED INTO A WOODEN BOX, WITH SOME WATER AND A FEW BISCUITS.

HE MADE HOLES TO BREATHE THROUGH AND BROUGHT A DRILL IN CASE HE NEEDED TO MAKE MORE AIR HOLES ALONG THE WAY.

"BEING THUS EQUIPPED FOR THE BATTLE OF LIBERTY," BROWN LATER WROTE, "MY FRIENDS NAILED DOWN THE LID . . ."

", . . AND HAD ME CONVEYED TO THE EXPRESS OFFICE, WHICH WAS ABOUT A MILE DISTANT FROM THE PLACE WHERE I WAS PACKED."

"I HAD NO SOONER ARRIVED AT THE OFFICE THAN I WAS TURNED HEELS UP, WHILE SOME PERSON NAILED SOMETHING ON THE END OF THE BOX."

"I FELT MY EYES SWELLING AS IF THEY WOULD BURST FROM THEIR SOCKETS; AND THE VEINS ON MY TEMPLES WERE DREADFULLY DISTENDED WITH PRESSURE OF BLOOD UPON MY HEAD."

BROWN SPENT MORE THAN TWENTY-SIX HOURS INSIDE THE BOX, TRAVELING BY WAGON, BOAT, AND TRAIN, ALL THE WAY TO PHILADELPHIA.

WILLIAM STILL AND OTHER ANTISLAVERY ACTIVISTS WERE WAITING FOR HIM.

IS ALL RIGHT WITHIN?

ALL RIGHT.

THE ABOLITIONISTS USED A SAW AND HATCHET TO PRY OPEN THE BOX . . .

. . . AND OUT POPPED HENRY BROWN.

HOW DO YOU DO, GENTLEMEN?

HE WAS SO RELIEVED TO HAVE MADE IT THAT HE SANG A HYMN.

OTHER ANTISLAVERY ACTIVISTS WELCOMED BROWN WITH FOOD AND FRESH CLOTHES AND HELPED HIM MAKE HIS WAY TO BOSTON TO LIVE AS A FREE MAN.

BROWN LATER TOLD HIS STORY AT ANTISLAVERY MEETINGS AND IN FRONT OF OTHER GROUPS, WHICH HELPED GAIN MORE SUPPORT FOR THE ABOLITIONIST MOVEMENT.

Henry Box Brown's story is among the most famous in the history of the Underground Railroad, but he wasn't the only person who tried to escape from slavery in a box. In 1859, William Peel had friends box him up and load him onto a steamer bound for Philadelphia. A friend traveled ahead to meet Peel when he arrived, but getting him to a safe house was another challenge. It turned out that the box didn't fit in the carriage his friend had brought, so he had to find another one. While he was loading the box into that one, Peel coughed and was almost discovered.

COUGH, COUGH

But they made it to safety, and after seventeen hours cooped up in that box, Peel climbed out. Eventually, he made it to Canada.

William Still's book also describes a woman who escaped from slavery in a box in 1857. She arrived in Philadelphia barely able to walk. She'd been breathing through a tiny hole she poked in the box with a pair of scissors.

This type of escape carried huge risks. Samuel Smith, the white man who helped Henry Brown escape, tried to do the same with two other enslaved people and got caught. Smith was arrested and thrown in prison, and the two people he'd tried to help were sent back to slavery.

And in 1860, two Nashville men tried to send a box to Cincinnati abolitionist Levi Coffin. It was supposed to be sent by train to Kentucky, ferried across the Ohio River, and then put on two more trains until it reached Cincinnati. But at a train station in Indiana, somebody threw the box onto the platform, and when it broke open, a Black man fell out. He'd been cooped up fourteen hours with nothing to eat or drink. Police took him to jail and then sent him back to slavery in Nashville.

HISTORIANS BELIEVE MOST PEOPLE WHO TRIED TO ESCAPE ENDED UP ENSLAVED AGAIN, BUT STILL'S BOOK IS FULL OF THE DARING STORIES OF THOSE WHO MADE IT NORTH.

THERE WAS LEAR GREEN, A YOUNG WOMAN WHO ESCAPED IN A WOODEN SAILOR'S CHEST . . .

. . . AND ROBERT BROWN, WHO CROSSED THE POTOMAC RIVER ON HORSEBACK IN A STORM ON CHRISTMAS NIGHT.

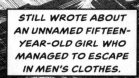

STILL WROTE ABOUT AN UNNAMED FIFTEEN-YEAR-OLD GIRL WHO MANAGED TO ESCAPE IN MEN'S CLOTHES.

HE DESCRIBED HOW CHARLES GILBERT ESCAPED FROM A VIRGINIA SLAVE TRADER . . .

. . . AND ASKED A SHIP CAPTAIN TO HELP HIM. THE CAPTAIN SAID SURE, AS LONG AS GILBERT COULD MAKE IT TO THE DOCK HE PLANNED TO LEAVE FROM. IT WAS 160 MILES AWAY.

THE WHOLE THING WAS A SETUP. THE CAPTAIN KNEW GILBERT HAD RELATIVES IN THAT TOWN AND LIKELY TOLD AUTHORITIES TO LOOK FOR HIM THERE. SOMEONE WARNED GILBERT TO STAY OUT OF SIGHT, SO HE HID IN EVERY WAY IMAGINABLE. FIRST, HE HOLED UP UNDER A HOTEL . . .

. . . FOR FOUR WEEKS!

BUT THEN SOMEONE DISCOVERED HIS HIDING PLACE.

GILBERT FLED TO THE WOODS AND HID IN A TREE FOR A DAY.

WHEN HE CAME DOWN, A WOMAN HID HIM UNDER THE FLOOR OF A WASHHOUSE FOR TWO WEEKS.

WHEN OFFICERS CAME TO SEARCH, GILBERT HIGHTAILED IT BACK TO THE HOTEL.

HE HID IN A THICKET . . .

. . . AND IN A MARSH.

POOR GILBERT KEPT BOUNCING AROUND UNTIL HIS FAMILY RAISED MONEY TO BUY HIM PASSAGE ON A STEAMBOAT.

BUT BEFORE HE COULD GET AWAY, OFFICIALS CAME SEARCHING AGAIN.

GILBERT HAD TO THINK FAST! HE FOUND SOME WOMEN'S CLOTHES TO DISGUISE HIMSELF.

WHOSE GAL ARE YOU?

MR. COCKLING'S, SIR.

WHAT IS YOUR NAME?

DELIE, SIR.

GO ON, THEN!

SO GILBERT LEFT AND HEADED FOR THE STEAMER.

THE SHIP TOOK HIM TO NORFOLK, VIRGINIA, WHERE HE HAD TO HIDE OUT FOR ANOTHER FOUR WEEKS BEFORE FINALLY MAKING IT TO PHILADELPHIA AND FREEDOM.

Most often, William Still helped strangers and recorded their stories. But one day, a man walked into Still's office and explained that he'd purchased his freedom and wanted help finding his family. That man turned out to be Peter Still—William's own brother, who'd been left behind in slavery when his mother had escaped forty years earlier. William Still was able to find his brother's wife and children and secure the money needed to free them.

Still was one of the most famous conductors of the Underground Railroad, second only to the woman whose story appears in almost every history book about this time period—Harriet Tubman. She wasn't always called Harriet, but she was always brave. Born to enslaved parents, she was originally named Araminta Ross and called Minty. She married a free man named John Tubman and changed her first name to Harriet, which was her mother's name, too.

After Harriet Tubman escaped from slavery and fled to Philadelphia in 1849, she regularly went back to Maryland to rescue family and friends, risking her life and freedom every time. Stories about Tubman have spread far and wide, but only some of them are true. Others need a little smashing.

THE STORY: Harriet Tubman rescued more than three hundred people on nineteen trips all over the South.

THE REAL DEAL: There's no doubt that Harriet Tubman was amazing and brave, but that number may be an exaggeration. Historians who have studied Tubman's own speeches and other historical documents say there's evidence that she rescued at least fifty to seventy people. And she did provide information that helped many others find their way to freedom. But she didn't travel throughout the South; her rescues were all in Maryland.

Famous photographs of Harriet Tubman taken later in her life sometimes lead people to imagine her as a sweet old woman, quietly helping enslaved people escape. But Harriet was younger and absolutely fierce while she was doing that work. She reportedly carried a drug to quiet crying babies and a gun to defend against slave hunters. She also threatened to use it if those in her care thought about turning back. She wouldn't allow anyone to run off and give away information that could put the whole group at risk.

DID SHE REALLY SAY THAT?

People admire Harriet Tubman and like to share inspirational things they think she said.

> IF YOU ARE TIRED, KEEP GOING.
> IF YOU ARE SCARED, KEEP GOING.
> IF YOU ARE HUNGRY, KEEP GOING.
> IF YOU WANT TO TASTE FREEDOM, KEEP GOING.
> —HARRIET TUBMAN?

That's the sort of quote that makes you want to cheer, isn't it? Keep going! The trouble is, there's no evidence that those words ever came out of Harriet Tubman's mouth.

It's possible that she said something like that at some point in her life, but the words don't appear in any primary sources. Historians believe the quote first showed up in a book about Tubman in the 1950s, and people likely accepted it as fact because it sounds like something she might have said and certainly fit her spirit.

SIGNAL LANTERNS AND FREEDOM QUILTS

Some stories about the Underground Railroad say enslaved people could spot a safe house by a lantern in the window or a specially coded quilt on a clothesline. Those tales are rooted in oral history, but some are a little shaky. There *was* a well-known antislavery activist named John Rankin, who lived on the Ohio River and sometimes used a lantern to signal to freedom seekers when it was safe for them to cross. But lanterns were not widely used to identify Underground Railroad safe houses. (If they had been, those houses would have been easy for slave hunters to find, too.)

So what about those legendary Underground Railroad quilts?

According to stories, these quilts were full of secret symbols. A bow tie suggested that enslaved people should try to dress to look wealthy. A bear paw told them to follow animal trails to find food and water. A log cabin was a sign that a house was a safe place to

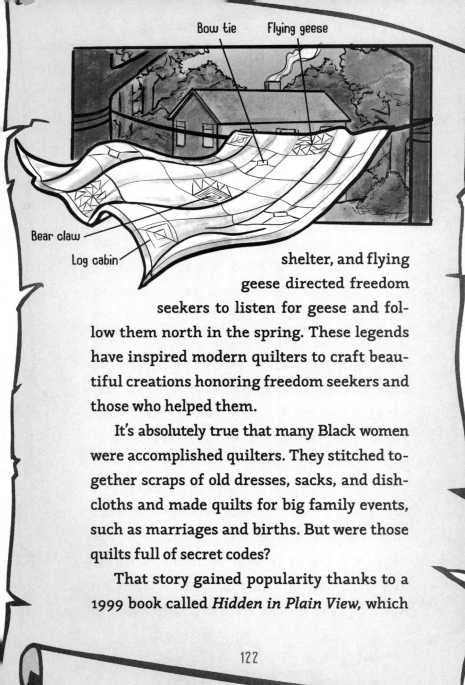

Bow tie   Flying geese

Bear claw

Log cabin

shelter, and flying geese directed freedom seekers to listen for geese and follow them north in the spring. These legends have inspired modern quilters to craft beautiful creations honoring freedom seekers and those who helped them.

It's absolutely true that many Black women were accomplished quilters. They stitched together scraps of old dresses, sacks, and dishcloths and made quilts for big family events, such as marriages and births. But were those quilts full of secret codes?

That story gained popularity thanks to a 1999 book called *Hidden in Plain View*, which was based on oral histories from a family the authors interviewed. Historians looking for evidence to support the book's claims didn't come up with much in the way of official documents, so we can't prove that coded quilts were in widespread use.

But we also can't prove that they *weren't* part of the Underground Railroad story. Historians recognize that oral histories are also an important part of the historical record, especially when it comes to African American families. Most enslaved people were forbidden to learn to read or write, and their family histories were largely erased by slavery. However common coded quilts may have been during the days of slavery, the quilts have become an important symbol of hope and a way for descendants of enslaved people to honor the memory of their ancestors.

EIGHT
AN UNJUST LAW

William Still and other abolitionists paid close attention to different states' laws about slavery. Sometimes they could use those laws to help free people.

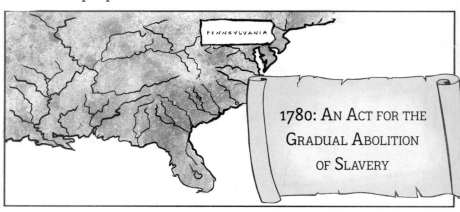

PENNSYLVANIA

1780: An Act for the Gradual Abolition of Slavery

Pennsylvania had started getting rid of slavery in 1780. With the law passed that year, no one was required to free the people they had already enslaved, but all children born in Pennsylvania would be free, and no more enslaved people could be imported into the state. Anyone who visited Pennsylvania and brought enslaved people with them was allowed to keep them enslaved there for up to six months. After that, they would be freed.

THE PRESIDENT'S PROBLEM

Pennsylvania's Act for the Gradual Abolition of Slavery created a bit of a problem for

America's new president, George Washington. Philadelphia became the nation's temporary capital in 1790. When Washington moved there, he wanted to bring along some of the people he had enslaved on his plantation in Virginia. To get around the law, about every six months, Washington would take the enslaved people back to Mount Vernon or on another trip out of the state. That reset the clock on their freedom so he could keep them enslaved.

Legal slavery in Pennsylvania ended in 1847. The new law meant that any enslaved people who were brought to Pennsylvania were automatically free when they arrived in the state. Most enslavers knew this and stopped bringing enslaved people north. But others either weren't paying attention or just didn't think anyone would notice, so they brought enslaved people to Pennsylvania anyway. When that happened, William Still and others in the Philadelphia Vigilance Committee made it their business to let people know about the law. They'd seek out enslaved visitors, tell them they were entitled to freedom, and ask if they wanted help.

STILL RUSHED THE NOTE TO THE OFFICE OF ANOTHER ANTISLAVERY ACTIVIST, NAMED PASSMORE WILLIAMSON. THEN HE RACED TO THE HOTEL.

A TALL, DARK WOMAN, WITH TWO LITTLE BOYS . . .

BUT THE ENSLAVED PEOPLE HAD ALREADY LEFT TO BOARD A BOAT.

STILL HURRIED TO THE DOCK. WILLIAMSON SHOWED UP THERE, TOO. AT FIRST, THEY COULDN'T FIND THE WOMAN AND HER SONS.

THEY ARE UP ON THE SECOND DOCK!

ARE YOU TRAVELING?

YES.

WITH WHOM?

DO THEY BELONG TO YOU, SIR?

YES, THEY ARE IN MY CHARGE.

YOU ARE ENTITLED TO YOUR FREEDOM ACCORDING TO THE LAWS OF PENNSYLVANIA, HAVING BEEN BROUGHT INTO THE STATE BY YOUR OWNER. . . . ACT CALMLY—DON'T BE FRIGHTENED BY YOUR MASTER—YOU ARE AS MUCH ENTITLED TO YOUR FREEDOM AS WE ARE, OR AS HE IS.

REMEMBER, IF YOU LOSE THIS CHANCE YOU MAY NEVER GET SUCH ANOTHER.

THEN THE ENSLAVER STEPPED IN. HE SAID JOHNSON WAS ON A VISIT TO SEE FRIENDS AND WANTED TO RETURN TO VIRGINIA WITH HIM AFTER THAT TO SEE HER OTHER CHILDREN.

HE PRESSED HER TO AGREE WITH HIM: THAT WAS TRUE. WASN'T IT?

I AM NOT FREE, BUT I WANT MY FREEDOM—ALWAYS WANTED TO BE FREE!

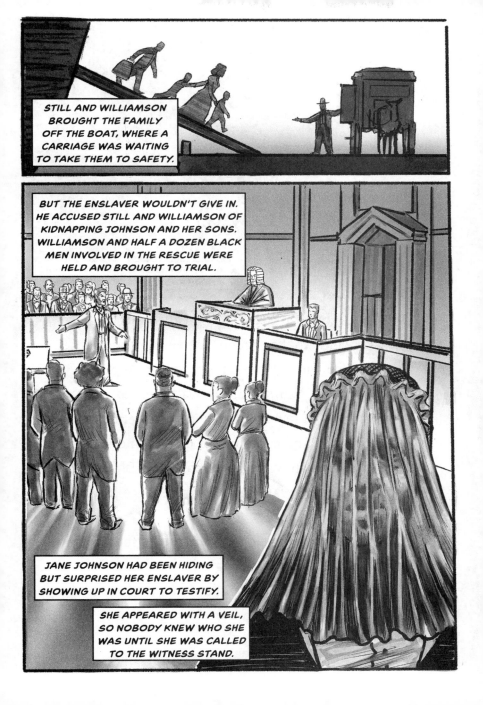

THERE, SHE MADE IT CLEAR THAT HER ENSLAVER WAS LYING.

NOBODY FORCED ME AWAY; NOBODY PULLED ME, AND NOBODY LED ME; I WENT AWAY OF MY OWN FREE WILL; I ALWAYS WISHED TO BE FREE AND MEANT TO BE FREE WHEN I CAME NORTH.

AFTER JOHNSON'S TESTIMONY, SHE WAS RUSHED BACK TO SAFETY.

You might think that being called out as a liar like that would make that enslaver give up and call it a day. But he and his pro-slavery lawyers kept at it.

Eventually, William Still was cleared of any crime, though a few of the other men spent time in jail for assault and contempt of court. Jane Johnson escaped to Boston, where she married a Black man, and their home became another safe place for those escaping from slavery.

Johnson wasn't the only woman who found freedom when her enslaver brought her to Pennsylvania. In 1859, the Philadelphia Vigilance Committee heard that Cordelia Loney, who was enslaved by a wealthy woman staying at a local boardinghouse, wanted to be free. Committee members got word to Loney that she was allowed to go, so she packed up her trunk and left. Still wrote that Loney was happy to learn her enslaver was having a tough time without her.

"After leaving her mistress she learned, with no little degree of pleasure, that a perplexed state of things existed at the boarding-house; that her mistress was seriously puzzled to imagine how she would get her shoes and stockings on and off; how she would get her head combed, get dressed, be attended to in sickness, etc."

—WILLIAM STILL, *THE UNDERGROUND RAILROAD RECORDS*

The other wealthy white enslavers felt awful for the woman. A white pastor in town asked a Black man he knew to help find Loney. The minister explained how nicely that enslaver treated her servants. He said Loney would never be able to take care of herself anyway, so the man would probably be doing her a favor if he ratted her out. That Black man was Thomas Dorsey, a Philadelphia caterer who'd been enslaved himself and escaped. So he knew the truth. He told the minister that Loney had every right to be free and said he wouldn't give up her location even if he knew it. Loney escaped to Canada.

FLAUNTING FREEDOM

Most enslaved people who escaped simply wanted to disappear and live their lives as free people. But a few wanted to make sure their enslavers knew they'd made it and were doing just fine without them. Sometimes, they even posted notices in newspapers.

Tell Mary Wrightson, Cook's Point, Maryland, that Moses Giles wishes to be remembered to her as an old acquaintance, and that he was well and in good spirits, and liked liberty very much.

Henry Hawkins would like to have Sam inform Austin Scott, at Washington City, that he is well, and is delighted with Northern scenery and society, and hopes he may get along without his services in the future. He wants him to send the editor of the Tocsin money enough to buy a new coat, as the linen roundabout is very nearly worn out, and it is coming on cold soon. This would only be a *very* small item in the amount of which Scott has robbed him of his services.

In other words: **Please let our enslavers know we made it to freedom—and they can't control our lives anymore.**

In early 1850, lawmakers in the South introduced legislation that would set up new rules for returning people to slavery after they escaped. At that time, people from the South weren't allowed to bring those they enslaved into northern free states without those people being freed. Kentucky senator Henry Clay said the North was just being unkind and unneighborly. Imagine forcing people to travel without enslaved servants!

The debate over the new law was fierce. It was more than a decade before the Civil War would begin, but there were already worries that the South might secede, or break away, from the rest of the country over the issue of slavery. Finally, the Fugitive Slave Act of 1850 passed that summer. The new law created a special position—US commissioners who would be appointed by federal judges. They'd hear cases about fugitive slaves and issue certificates of removal, papers that allowed enslaved people who escaped to the North to be returned to slavery. The commissioners' orders would be final and couldn't be challenged in any other court.

The whole system was set up to be unfair. For starters, a commissioner got paid five dollars for hearing the case if he sided with the person who'd escaped from slavery and *twice that* if he ruled in favor of the enslaver. Enslaved people weren't even allowed to defend themselves in court. And the law was retroactive, which meant that people who had escaped from slavery in the past and had been living in the North for years could still be recaptured. Even free Black people were at risk of being kidnapped off the streets and enslaved. Warning posters went up in cities to let Black people know of the danger.

CAUTION!!

COLORED PEOPLE

OF BOSTON, ONE & ALL,

You are hereby respectfully CAUTIONED and advised, to avoid conversing with the

Watchmen and Police Officers of Boston,

For since the recent ORDER OF THE MAYOR & ALDERMEN, they are empowered to act as

KIDNAPPERS

AND

Slave Catchers,

And they have already been actually employed in KIDNAPPING, CATCHING, AND KEEPING SLAVES. Therefore, if you value your LIBERTY, and the *Welfare of the Fugitives* among you, *Shun* them in every possible manner, as so many *HOUNDS* on the track of the most unfortunate of your race.

Keep a Sharp Look Out for KIDNAPPERS, and have TOP EYE open.

APRIL 24, 1851.

THE STORY OF SOLOMON NORTHUP

After the Fugitive Slave Act was passed, free Black people weren't even safe walking the streets of their own cities. Solomon Northup lived the horror of being a free Black man who suddenly found himself enslaved.

An engraving from Solomon Northup's autobiography, *Twelve Years a Slave*

Northup could read and write, and he was a talented fiddle player. He'd married a free woman named Anne Hampton and was living with her and their three children in Saratoga Springs, New York. In March 1841, two men approached Northup while he was away from his home. They offered him a job playing fiddle for their circus act. But when Northup traveled to Washington, DC, where slavery was still legal, the men drugged him and sold him into slavery in New Orleans.

There, no one cared about Northup's claims that he was free. He was strong and able to work in the fields. So that's what Northup was forced to do—for *twelve years!* Finally, he met someone who was able to get word to New York about what had happened to him, and his family and friends worked to rescue him. After Northup returned to New York, he wrote his autobiography, a now-famous book called *Twelve Years a Slave.*

The Fugitive Slave Act overruled all local and state laws in the North. Local people could even be forced to help officers enforce the law. Anyone who aided enslaved people in an escape could be fined or thrown in prison. You might think those threats would have put a quick end to the activities of the Underground Railroad, but they didn't. They just made antislavery activists fight back harder.

NINE
DARING AND DEFIANCE

The Fugitive Slave Act was meant to make life easier for enslavers, but it just fired up anti-slavery activists even more. People who broke the new law understood that they were fighting injustice. Many northern lawmakers spoke out against it.

"In the long catalogue of public crimes among civilized nations, there is none more cruel and barbarous than the Fugitive Slave Law."

—WISCONSIN CONGRESSMAN
CHARLES DURKEE

" *It must have been expected that so infamous a law would have been evaded by underground railroads, and by all other honorable methods. . . . All parties wink at its evasion, and all sympathy is with the fugitive.*"
—NEW YORK CONGRESSMAN CHARLES B. SEDGWICK

In other words: Nobody here wants to enforce this rotten law, and everyone is on the side of the enslaved people.

The first person to be arrested under the new law was a man named James Hamlet, who lived in Brooklyn. Hamlet's enslaver, a Maryland woman named Mary Brown, hired a police firm to capture him. Officers found out where he was, waited for the new law to take effect, and then showed up in New York. Before his hearing, Hamlet had told people that he was legally a free man because his parents had been freed from slavery. But he wasn't allowed to testify. The commissioner ordered Hamlet to be sent back to slavery, so federal marshals handcuffed him and put him on a boat headed for Baltimore.

People in New York were furious. They learned that Hamlet's enslaver had offered to let him buy his freedom for eight hundred dollars. So two thousand free Black people came together to raise money for his release. A newspaper pitched in to help with fundraising, too, and a local merchant took the money to Baltimore. Hamlet was back in New York within a week, and thousands of people gathered at City Hall Park in Manhattan to celebrate his return.

Harriet Jacobs had escaped from slavery in North Carolina in 1842. She lived as a free woman in the North for years, but when the new law was passed, her whole life changed.

"All that winter I lived in a state of anxiety. When I took the children out to breathe the air, I closely observed the countenances of all I met. I dreaded the approach of summer, when snakes and slaveholders made their appearance."

—HARRIET JACOBS, *INCIDENTS IN THE LIFE OF A SLAVE GIRL*, 1861

William and Ellen Craft had escaped from Macon, Georgia, in 1848. Ellen, who was light-skinned, disguised herself as a white man and acted as if her husband were an enslaved servant as the two traveled north.

Illustrations of Ellen and William Craft from the
antislavery newspaper the *Liberator*

They kept up the act the whole way and even stayed overnight at a first-class hotel in Charleston, South Carolina. When they made it to Boston, they published the story of their daring escape.

But after the Fugitive Slave Act was passed, cities were full of slave catchers who made money by collecting rewards for capturing freedom seekers. Some people in Boston fought those who were trying to enforce the new law. They put up posters so people could identify slave catchers and harass them on the streets. Eventually, the slave catchers who had come searching for William and Ellen Craft left town, and the Crafts went on to England.

Other people fled to Canada to avoid being captured or kidnapped. In the 1840s, some Black settlements were established in the part of Canada that's now called Ontario. In Canada, free Black men had more rights than they did in the United States. They were allowed to serve on juries, testify in court, and vote.

In the decade after the Fugitive Slave Act was passed, about three hundred enslaved people who had escaped were captured from northern states and returned to slavery. That number might have been a lot higher if it weren't for the efforts of free Black people who made life difficult—and unsafe—for slave catchers. At antislavery meetings throughout the North, activists argued that the new law was evil, and that justified the use of violence to fight it.

"*The only way to make the Fugitive Slave Law a dead letter is to make half a dozen or more dead kidnappers.*"

—FREDERICK DOUGLASS,
AT THE 1852 CONVENTION OF THE
FREE SOIL PARTY

The battle against this unjust law began almost as soon as it was passed. In October 1850, when an enslaved man who had escaped was arrested in Detroit, hundreds of armed Black people showed up at the jail where he was being held. The enslaver quickly backed down and allowed the man to be purchased and freed.

Shadrach Minkins, another man who'd escaped from slavery, was working at a Boston coffeehouse when federal marshals took him into custody in February 1851. He was the first person in Massachusetts to be arrested under the Fugitive Slave Act, and it didn't take long for word to get out. While the case was being heard in court, about twenty other Black men stormed into the courthouse and literally carried Minkins out the door. Abolitionist Lewis Hayden hid Minkins until he could escape to Canada six days later.

The following year, a group of antislavery activists fought off slave catchers who showed up searching for people who had escaped to Christiana, Pennsylvania.

IN SEPTEMBER 1851, WILLIAM PARKER WAS SHELTERING SEVERAL FREEDOM SEEKERS IN HIS FARMHOUSE WHEN THEIR ENSLAVER, EDWARD GORSUCH, SHOWED UP FROM MARYLAND WITH OTHER WHITE MEN.

THE MEN SURROUNDED PARKER'S HOUSE.

A FEDERAL MARSHAL DEMANDED THAT THE PEOPLE WHO HAD ESCAPED BE TURNED OVER TO HIM.

BUT PARKER AND THE OTHERS BARRICADED THEMSELVES ON THE SECOND FLOOR. THEY HAD WEAPONS TO DEFEND THEMSELVES.

AS THE SITUATION GREW MORE HEATED, ELIZA PARKER, WILLIAM'S WIFE, BLEW A HORN OUT THE WINDOW TO CALL FOR HELP.

NEIGHBORS HAD BEEN WARNED THAT SLAVE CATCHERS MIGHT SHOW UP. THEY WERE READY. AND WHEN THE ALARM WENT OUT . . .

. . . THEY SHOWED UP WITH GUNS, AXES, CORN CUTTERS, AND CLUBS, READY TO DEFEND THEIR FRIENDS.

SHOTS WERE FIRED. THE ENSLAVER ONCE AGAIN DEMANDED THAT THE MEN WHO'D ESCAPED BE TURNED OVER.

YOU'D BETTER GO AWAY IF YOU DON'T WANT TO GET HURT!

THE SLAVE CATCHERS FLED TO THE WOODS. BUT NOT BEFORE THE ENSLAVER HAD BEEN KILLED AND HIS SON WOUNDED.

WHEN IT WAS OVER, THE PEOPLE WHO'D JUST HAD TO FIGHT FOR THEIR NEIGHBORS' LIVES HELPED THE WOUNDED MAN LEFT BEHIND.

After the violence in Christiana, William Parker and others who were involved fled to Canada. The US government charged them with treason but couldn't arrest them, because Canada protected people who had escaped from slavery. The fighting came to be known as the Christiana Riot. It sent a strong message to those who still supported slavery: don't expect to show up in the North and not be challenged.

William Still wrote that things were a little different after Christiana.

"*Slave-holders from Maryland especially were far less disposed to hunt their runaway property than they had hitherto been. The Deputy Marshal likewise considered the business of catching slaves very unsafe.*"

—WILLIAM STILL,
THE UNDERGROUND
RAILROAD RECORDS

Southern enslavers still sent men north to try to capture people who escaped. But more and more often, slave catchers were met with antislavery activists who were prepared and committed to justice.

A month after the Christiana Riot, slave catchers in Syracuse, New York, faced similar resistance when they captured Jerry McHenry, who had escaped from slavery in North Carolina eight years earlier. Antislavery activists in town for a convention found out what had happened. It was a mixed crowd—Black people and white people, lawyers, ministers, doctors, and tradesmen who worked with their hands. Together, they stormed the police station to rescue Jerry McHenry, who then escaped to Canada.

Stories like this always made the newspapers. Abolitionists wanted word to get out that anyone who tried to deny people freedom wouldn't be safe. And it was at least somewhat effective. Efforts to fight off slave catchers weren't always successful, but the fact that abolitionists worked so hard to defend freedom seekers who were arrested—and the fact that many were willing to resort to violence to defend their fellow citizens—made the Fugitive Slave Act an expensive and dangerous law to enforce.

ABRAHAM LINCOLN: TAKING A STAND?

When people think about the end of slavery in the United States, Abraham Lincoln is often one of the first names that comes to mind. So you might imagine that good old Abe was right in there fighting for justice with other antislavery activists from day one. But you'd be wrong about that. Some people were willing to break the law to help enslaved people, but Lincoln wasn't one of them.

In 1855, he wrote a letter to his friend Joshua Speed, who had grown up on a plantation and still enslaved people. Lincoln talked about their different views and assured Speed that even though Lincoln wasn't a fan of slavery, he wasn't suggesting that Speed be forced to free anyone.

" I confess I hate to see the poor creatures hunted down, and caught, and carried back to their stripes, and unrewarded toils; but I bite my lip and keep quiet."

—LETTER FROM ABRAHAM LINCOLN TO JOSHUA SPEED, AUGUST 24, 1855

In other words: Slavery sure does seem wrong, but I'm not ready to speak up about that yet.

But Lincoln was clearly uncomfortable with the whole situation. The Fugitive Slave Act had made more white people feel that way, and some changed their views as a result. Lincoln's views about his own responsibilities would evolve, too. Eventually, he'd play a role in finally changing the laws that for hundreds of years had allowed one American to enslave another.

TEN
SLAVERY ENDS . . .
BUT ITS LEGACY LIVES ON

You've probably read in history books how the Union won the Civil War and put an end to slavery in the United States. That's true, but a whole series of events led up to that change.

The Fugitive Slave Act of 1850 and efforts to resist it turned up the heat in the battle over slavery. There were fierce debates over where slavery should be allowed as new states were added to the United States, and arguments about the rights of free Black people as well as those who were enslaved. It all came to a head when the case of a man named Dred Scott went all the way to the Supreme Court, the highest court in the land.

Dred Scott and his wife, Harriet Robinson Scott, were enslaved in Missouri but were taken for a time to the free state of Illinois and the Wisconsin Territory, where slavery was also against the law. Back in Missouri in 1846, they filed lawsuits, claiming that because they'd been taken to places where slavery was illegal, they were automatically free. They couldn't be enslaved again just because they went back to a state that allowed it.

The case wound its way through the justice system for ten years, and different courts issued different rulings. The Scotts were enslaved! No, they were free! No, they were enslaved! Finally, the case went all the way to the US Supreme Court, and the chief justice announced a decision that was devastating for African Americans.

The court ruled against the Scotts and said they had no right to sue in the first place because people of African descent *weren't even American citizens.* The justices also upheld enslavers' rights and said Congress had no power to limit slavery in Missouri or anywhere else. Abolitionists were furious, and their movement continued to grow.

JOHN BROWN'S RAID

In October 1859, abolitionist John Brown led a group of men in a daring raid on the federal arsenal, a place where weapons were stored, at Harpers Ferry, Virginia. His plan was to have enslaved people take the weapons kept there  and start a freedom movement that would spread through the South. Brown seized the armory, but by the time his men took control, a local militia had surrounded the building. The two sides traded gunfire, and ten of Brown's followers were killed. The US military moved in the next day and arrested the abolitionists who were still alive.

Brown was executed for treason but became a hero to others fighting slavery. This infuriated people in the South, who couldn't understand how anyone could defend Brown. The two sides saw the events of Harpers Ferry totally differently—and grew even further apart.

The divide between northern and southern states felt impossible to bridge. After Abraham Lincoln was elected president in 1860, seven southern states seceded from the rest of the nation to create the Confederate States of America. The Civil War began the month after Lincoln was sworn into office, with Union troops of the North fighting Confederate troops of the South.

Many people who had been resisting slavery in various ways signed up to fight. Remember Captain Fountain from William Still's book? He signed up to be a Union soldier after Confederates burned his boat.

Harriet Tubman joined the Union army, too. Officially, she was working as a cook and a nurse, but really, she was acting as a spy!

In 1863, Tubman guided Union gunboats full of Black soldiers on a raid to disrupt Confederate supply lines and free over seven hundred enslaved people.

The Union army recruited enslaved African Americans to join them and essentially became the new Underground Railroad. More than ninety thousand men escaped and joined the army to help the North win the Civil War. Even some people who had fled to Canada to escape slavery returned so they could enlist.

By the end of 1861, Lincoln had declared that any enslaved people who reached Union lines were free, and the following year, Congress prohibited soldiers from returning anyone to slavery. The war had created what the antislavery newspaper the *Liberator* called a "National Underground Railroad."

On New Year's Day 1863, Abraham Lincoln issued the Emancipation Proclamation. Lots of books describe this as the day Lincoln "freed the slaves." But that's not the whole story. When enslaved people in Confederate states were declared free on January 1, 1863, Union soldiers marched through the South reading copies of the document to spread the word. But in some areas that were still under Confederate control, enslaved people were refused freedom until much later.

It wasn't until June 19, 1865, that Union troops made their way to Galveston, Texas, and announced that more than a quarter of a million people enslaved in the state were finally free. That date came to be known as Juneteenth and was declared a national holiday in 2021.

President Joe Biden signed the National Independence Day Act on June 17, 2021.

The Emancipation Proclamation declared that enslaved people living in Confederate states were free, but slavery wasn't actually abolished until the Thirteenth Amendment to the Constitution was ratified in December 1865.

THIRTEENTH AMENDMENT

Neither slavery nor involuntary servitude, except as a punishment for crime whereof the party shall have been duly convicted, shall exist within the United States, or any place subject to their jurisdiction.

HEY, MISSISSIPPI!
YOU FORGOT SOMETHING . . .

To become law, a constitutional amendment has to be approved by two-thirds of both houses of Congress and by three-quarters of the states. Most states ratified, or approved, the Thirteenth Amendment in 1865, and it became law at that time. But some states took a lot longer to vote yes.

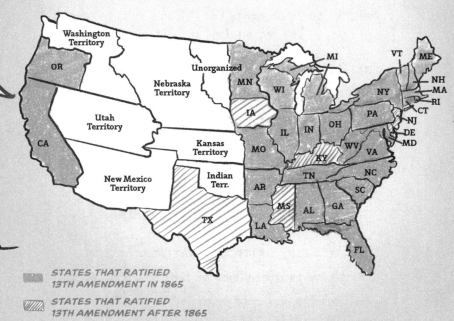

STATES THAT RATIFIED
13TH AMENDMENT IN 1865

STATES THAT RATIFIED
13TH AMENDMENT AFTER 1865

TERRITORIES THAT WEREN'T STATES YET IN 1865

Mississippi didn't officially vote to ban slavery until 1995, more than a hundred years after the Civil War ended. That's when the state's lawmakers finally approved the amendment. But even then, Mississippi's secretary of state never reported the vote to the federal register, so it wasn't official. That oversight was corrected in 2013, and Mississippi became the last state to formally say no to slavery. While this seems shockingly overdue, it didn't actually change any laws. The amendment had already passed without Mississippi's help, and slavery had been outlawed since 1865, whether Mississippi liked it or not.

Even after slavery was abolished, Black people had to fight for equality. Two more amendments to the Constitution helped with that. The Fourteenth Amendment declared previously enslaved people to be US citizens, with all the protections of the Constitution, and the Fifteenth Amendment promised African American men the right to vote.

But racists fought back hard. Southern states passed Black Codes, which were laws that kept African Americans from being truly equal. Hate groups such as the Ku Klux Klan sprung up, pushing the racist idea that white people were superior to other races and committing acts of violence against people of color.

These white-supremacy groups—and the racism they promote—still exist in the United States today. They are just one example of slavery's harmful legacy.

MAKING A CASE FOR REPARATIONS

In recent years, many people in the United States have raised the idea of reparations for slavery, which means paying people to help make amends for harm that was done to them.

Because millions of Black Americans were enslaved and forced to work without pay for hundreds of years, they didn't have the opportunity to build wealth and pass that wealth on to their descendants. And because racism

persisted after slavery ended, African American people were also denied equal access to everything from voting to education, jobs, and housing.

Should the United States make some sort of payments to people whose ancestors were enslaved? Lawmakers have introduced a bill to take a closer look at this idea. The proposal, known as H.R. 40, calls for a commission that would work to identify how the US government supported slavery and what kinds of lasting negative effects it's had on African American people and society.

Working to fight racism today may be the best way to honor those who fought against slavery. The United States has also tried to preserve historical sites associated with the Underground Railroad. Some, like William Still's residence in Philadelphia, are well documented.

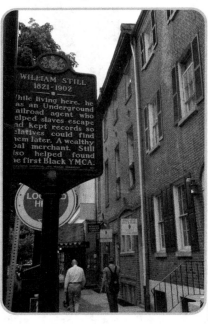

Others are harder to identify and confirm, though there's no shortage of stories about old houses rumored to have been part of the network. Families from free border states passed down these stories, whether or not there was any evidence to support them. The result is a whole lot of legends and not a lot of fact.

So how do historians figure out which stories are true? A project in Oswego County, New York, provides a glimpse of that process. In 1998, the National Park Service funded the project to find out if oral traditions—those family stories you hear about the Underground Railroad—could be documented through primary sources.

A team of researchers and volunteers started by making a big list of all the people and sites that might have somehow been connected to the Underground Railroad. They checked that list against articles in local history publications, nineteenth-century books about the Underground Railroad, and newspapers. Minutes of antislavery meetings and antislavery petitions also gave them names to consider. From there, they searched for personal letters, diaries, and obituaries to provide more evidence that those people listed were actually involved in the Underground Railroad. Sometimes they found proof.

The challenge in finding this sort of evidence is that many diaries were destroyed. Ohio abolitionist

December 24, 1850—
Today a colored man, his wife and five small girls
came to my house on their way to Canada to
save their children from kidnappers.

John Parker, who'd been enslaved himself, wrote that
he once kept a diary giving the names, dates, and cir-
cumstances of all the enslaved people he had helped.
But Parker had a family and owned a business, so he
had a lot to lose if he got caught.

Parker said this was a common practice after the
Fugitive Slave Act made it a crime to help people

"I threw this diary into the iron furnace, for fear it might fall into other hands."

—JOHN P. PARKER, *HIS PROMISED LAND: THE AUTOBIOGRAPHY OF JOHN P. PARKER, FORMER SLAVE AND CONDUCTOR ON THE UNDERGROUND RAILROAD*

escaping from slavery. If you were involved in that sort of work, the last thing you'd want was a list of all the crimes you'd committed, compiled for authorities in a nice, tidy notebook.

That's why finding evidence of the Underground Railroad has been such a challenge for historians. But they continue to locate documents and weigh the oral history of African American families, for whom keeping written records would have involved tremendous risk.

Their work led Congress to pass the National Underground Network to Freedom Act in 1998, to preserve historical sites and educate people. The sites include locations of famous court cases relating to the Underground Railroad as well as the sites of maroon communities in the Great Dismal Swamp and the Everglades. Together, these places help to tell the story of a shameful chapter in US history and the people from all different backgrounds who came together to fight injustice.

A TIMELINE OF SLAVERY AND THE UNDERGROUND RAILROAD

1619—The first enslaved Africans brought to the English colonies in America arrive in Jamestown.

1641—Massachusetts becomes the first colony to officially legalize slavery.

1712—A revolt of enslaved people in New York City results in the death of nine white men, followed by increased restrictions on enslaved people.

1739—Enslaved people in Stono, South Carolina, burn a firearms shop and kill at least twenty white people, in what's come to be called the Stono Rebellion. It is the largest uprising in the English colonies to date.

1754—Quakers in Pennsylvania publish an open letter against slavery.

1775—The Pennsylvania Society for Promoting the Abolition of Slavery is founded.

1776—The Declaration of Independence proclaims that "all men are created equal" but does not give rights to enslaved people. An early draft denounced slavery, but that line got revised out before it became official.

1777—Vermont becomes the first state to ban slavery and gives all adult males the right to vote.

1781—Elizabeth Freeman, also known as Mumbet, successfully sues her enslaver for her freedom. This helps lead to the end of legal slavery in Massachusetts.

1788—The US Constitution is ratified and guarantees enslavers the right to repossess any "person held to service or labor."

1793—Congress passes the first Fugitive Slave Act, making it a crime to help people who escaped from slavery or interfere with their arrests.

1793—Eli Whitney invents the cotton gin, a device that allows for large-scale production of cotton and increases the South's dependence on the labor of enslaved people.

1800—Gabriel Prosser leads a revolt of enslaved people in Richmond, Virginia. He's sentenced to death and killed, along with about twenty-five others who were involved. This leads states to pass new laws restricting movements of enslaved people.

1804—The Republic of Haiti is established after a revolt of enslaved people there.

1807—The international slave trade is outlawed in both Great Britain and the United States. However, the US domestic slave trade continues.

1816—The African Methodist Episcopal Church is organized, with Richard Allen as its bishop. It's the first all-Black religious denomination in the United States.

The American Colonization Society is founded to take free Black people and freed slaves to Africa. This leads to the creation of a colony that eventually becomes the Republic of Liberia in 1847.

1819—The attorney general of Upper Canada declares that enslaved people who arrive in Canada are free, paving the way for thousands of enslaved people to flee to Canada by the end of the Civil War.

1820—The Missouri Compromise leads to Missouri being admitted to the United States as a slave state, while Maine is admitted as a free state. Also, all western territories north of Missouri's southern border would be free from slavery.

1822—Denmark Vesey leads a rebellion of enslaved people in Charleston, South Carolina.

1826—Levi and Catharine Coffin help enslaved people escape by harboring them in their Indiana home for the first time. The Coffins may have helped more than two thousand enslaved people escape.

1829—Mexico abolishes slavery and becomes a refuge for people escaping from slave states in the United States.

1831—Nat Turner leads a rebellion of enslaved people in Southampton County, Virginia; about sixty white people are killed before the revolt is quashed by the militia.

William Lloyd Garrison founds an abolitionist newspaper called the *Liberator*.

1839—Enslaved people revolt on board the Spanish slave ship *Amistad* and land on Long Island.

1841—The US Supreme Court rules that the enslaved people on the *Amistad* were free people and had a right to resist "unlawful" slavery.

1845— *Narrative of the Life of Frederick Douglass*, the story of Douglass's escape and work in the abolition movement, is published.

1847—Frederick Douglass founds his abolitionist newspaper, the *North Star*.

1849—Henry Box Brown escapes from slavery by making arrangements to have himself mailed to abolitionists in Philadelphia.

Harriet Tubman escapes from slavery in Maryland, but soon returns to guide family members to freedom.

1850—The Compromise of 1850 brings California into the Union as a free state, bans public sales of enslaved people in Washington, DC, and allows enslavers to settle in lands seized from Mexico. It also establishes a new, tougher fugitive slave law and commits the government to enforce it, helping enslavers to capture people who escape.

1857—The Supreme Court's *Dred Scott* decision rules that Black people are not citizens of the United States and effectively overturns the Missouri Compromise, making all territories open to slavery.

1859—Abolitionist John Brown leads twenty-two men to raid the federal arsenal at Harpers Ferry, Virginia.

1860—Abraham Lincoln is elected president.

1861—The Civil War begins.

1863—Abraham Lincoln issues the Emancipation Proclamation, announcing that "slaves within any State or designated part of a State . . . in rebellion . . . shall be then, thenceforward, and forever free."

1865—After the Civil War ends, the Thirteenth Amendment outlaws slavery in the United States.

AUTHOR'S NOTE FROM GWENDOLYN HOOKS

Those who preferred to live in a swamp rather than be enslaved.

Those who were determined to fight for their freedom.

Those who taught others to read and write.

They are my heroes.

I admire each one of those heroes. Their lives were constantly in danger, but they didn't back down. Because of them, I am here to share their stories. And I'm very proud to do so.

As I researched these heroes, I reflected on my mother's side of our family tree. She was a country girl who grew up on a farm outside of Savannah, Georgia, with her brothers and sisters. Two sisters became teachers, and a brother was in the merchant marines. My mother married our air force father, who was from Oklahoma. They met when he was stationed in Savannah.

I was born in the military hospital in Savannah. But my sister, who is a year older, was not. She was born in the military hospital in Beaufort, South Carolina, about thirty miles away. Mother was not allowed in the Savannah facility at the time, because she was Black. How humiliating that must have been. The hospital's policy had changed by the time I was born. It explains why I have no memory of living in Beaufort. I do remember our Savannah house and our homes in Wichita Falls, Texas, and Tacoma, Washington, and even moments in Naples, Italy.

My mother and father were big believers in education. After dinner, we cleared the table and started on our homework. Not in our bedrooms but at the dining room table so they could keep an eye on us.

No homework? Find some! Luckily, we all loved school. And our proud parents saw their children graduate from college.

History Smashers: The Underground Railroad is the story of those who came before us and made our journey easier to navigate.

AUTHOR'S NOTE FROM KATE MESSNER

When I was growing up, my school history books were full of stories about the Underground Railroad. I learned about Harriet Tubman, but otherwise, the stories focused mostly on white Quakers who helped freedom seekers along the way. It was only when I was older that I read about the real horrors of slavery and learned that it was African Americans who did the most work—and took the greatest risks—to fight for justice. It's been an honor and a privilege to work with Gwen to share some of their stories in this book.

It can be challenging to write about a time period from which so much history was intentionally erased. There are also difficulties in accurately illustrating scenes from that history. While we have period photographs or portraits of Frederick Douglass, William

Still, Harriet Tubman, and many other historical figures, we simply don't know what others looked like. As a result, illustrations of some of the heroes in this book had to be imagined, based on the few details available in the historical record. They are all worth remembering and honoring. Here are some books, museums, and websites to explore if you'd like to learn more about the Underground Railroad and slavery's legacy of racism in the United States.

BOOKS

African Icons: Ten People Who Built a Continent by Tracey Baptiste, illustrated by Hillary Wilson (Algonquin, 2021)

The Amazing Age of John Roy Lynch by Chris Barton, illustrated by Don Tate (Eerdmans, 2015)

Before She Was Harriet by Lesa Cline-Ransome, illustrated by James E. Ransome (Holiday House, 2019)

Box: Henry Brown Mails Himself to Freedom by Carole Boston Weatherford, illustrated by Michele Wood (Candlewick, 2020)

Brick by Brick by Charles R. Smith Jr.; illustrated by Floyd Cooper (Amistad, 2015)

Freedom in Congo Square by Carole Boston Weatherford; illustrated by R. Gregory Christie (Little Bee Books, 2016)

Freedom Soup by Tami Charles; illustrated by Jacqueline Alcántara (Candlewick, 2019)

Let It Shine: Stories of Black Women Freedom Fighters by Andrea Davis Pinkney; illustrated by Stephen Alcorn (Houghton Mifflin Harcourt, 2013)

Moses: When Harriet Tubman Led Her People to Freedom by Carole Boston Weatherford; illustrated by Kadir Nelson (Hyperion, 2006)

Never Caught, The Story of Ona Judge: George and Martha Washington's Courageous Slave Who Dared to Run Away (Young Readers Edition) by Erica Armstrong Dunbar and Kathleen Van Cleve (Aladdin, 2019)

Ona Judge Outwits the Washingtons: An Enslaved Woman Fights for Freedom by Gwendolyn Hooks; illustrated by Simone Agoussoye (Capstone, 2019)

Stamped (For Kids): Racism, Antiracism, and You by Sonja Cherry-Paul, Jason Reynolds, and Ibram X. Kendi; illustrated by Rachelle Baker (Little, Brown, 2021)

William Still and His Freedom Stories: The Father of the Underground Railroad by Don Tate (Peachtree, 2020)

HISTORICAL SITES AND MUSEUMS

The Smithsonian's National Museum of African American History and Culture in Washington, DC, opened in 2016 and is the world's largest museum dedicated to African American history.

nmaahc.si.edu

The National Underground Railroad Freedom Center in Cincinnati, Ohio, tells the story of slavery in America and efforts to fight it.

freedomcenter.org

The Legacy Museum: From Enslavement to Mass Incarceration, in Montgomery, Alabama, explores the legacy of slavery and racism in America.

museumandmemorial.eji.org/museum

Rokeby Museum in Ferrisburgh, Vermont, was the home of an abolitionist family and is now a museum focused on the Underground Railroad.

rokeby.org

Whitney Plantation near Wallace, Louisiana, is a former sugarcane, rice, and indigo plantation that is now a museum focusing on the lives of enslaved people.

whitneyplantation.org

WEBSITES

Aboard the Underground Railroad: A National Register Travel Itinerary, from the National Park Service

nps.gov/nr/travel/underground

Africans in America, from PBS

pbs.org/wgbh/aia/home.html

Slavery in the United States: Primary Sources and the Historical Record, from the Library of Congress

**loc.gov/classroom-materials
/slavery-in-the-united-states-primary-sources-and-the
-historical-record/#students**

SELECTED BIBLIOGRAPHY

Bacon, Margaret Hope. "Robert Purvis: President of the Underground Railroad." *Pennsylvania Legacies* 5, no. 2 (November 2005): 15. jstor.org/stable/27764996.

Bell, Richard. *Stolen: Five Free Boys Kidnapped into Slavery and Their Astonishing Odyssey Home.* New York: 37 Ink, 2019.

Blackett, Richard. "The Underground Railroad and the Struggle Against Slavery." *History Workshop Journal* 78, no. 1 (August 8, 2014): 275–286.

Blight, David W. *Passages to Freedom: The Underground Railroad in History and Memory.* Washington, DC: Smithsonian Press, 2004.

Bordewich, Fergus M. *Bound for Canaan: The Epic Story of the Underground Railroad, America's First Civil Rights Movement.* New York: Amistad, 2006.

Brown, Henry Box. *Narrative of the Life of Henry Box Brown, Written by Himself.* Manchester, UK: Lee and Glynn, 1851. Online at Documenting the American South. docsouth.unc.edu/neh /brownbox/brownbox.html.

Bryant, Marie Claire. "Underground Railroad Quilt Codes: What We Know, What We Believe, and What Inspires Us." *Folklife,* May 3, 2019. folklife.si.edu/magazine/underground-railroad -quilt-codes.

Butler, M. B. *My Story of the Civil War and the Under-Ground Railroad.* Huntington, IN: United Brethren, 1914.

Butterworth, William. *Three Years Adventures of a Minor, in England, Africa, the West Indies, South-Carolina and Georgia.* Vol. 235. Leeds, UK: Baines, 1823.

Cecelski, David S. "The Shores of Freedom: The Maritime Underground Railroad in North Carolina, 1800–1861." *North Carolina Historical Review* 71, no. 2 (April 1994): 174–206. jstor.org/stable/23521582?seq=1.

Clavin, Matthew J. *Aiming for Pensacola: Fugitive Slaves on the Atlantic and Southern Frontiers.* Cambridge, MA: Harvard University Press, 2015.

Clavin, Matthew J. "'An Underground Railway' to Pensacola and the Impending Crisis over Slavery." *Florida Historical Quarterly* 92, no. 4 (Spring 2014) 685–713. jstor.org/stable/43488430.

Clinton, Catherine. *Harriet Tubman: The Road to Freedom.* New York: Back Bay Books, 2005.

Coates, Ta-Nehisi. "The Case for Reparations." *Atlantic,* June 2014. theatlantic.com/magazine/archive/2014/06/the-case-for -reparations/361631.

Coffin, Levi. *Reminiscences of Levi Coffin.* Cincinnati: Robert Clarke, 1880.

Contreras, Russell. "Story of the Underground Railroad to Mexico Gains Attention." Associated Press, September 16, 2020. apnews.com/article/mexico-race-and-ethnicity-archive-texas-d26243702f11e27b59b591332bb6775e.

Council, Ashley. "Ringing Liberty's Bell: African American Women, Gender, and the Underground Railroad in Philadelphia." *Pennsylvania History: A Journal of Mid-Atlantic Studies* 87, no. 3 (Summer 2020): 494–531. doi.org/10.5325/pennhistory.87.3.0494.

Crackel, Theodore J., ed. *The Papers of George Washington Digital Edition*. Charlottesville: University of Virginia Press, 2008. rotunda.upress.virginia.edu/founders/GEWN.html.

Delle, James. "In 1851, a Maryland Farmer Tried to Kidnap Free Blacks in Pennsylvania. He Wasn't Expecting the Neighborhood to Fight Back." *Smithsonian Magazine,* January 17, 2020. smithsonianmag.com/history/how-humble-stone-carries-memory-1851-african-american-uprising-against-fugitive-slave-law-180974003.

Delle, James A., and Jason Shellenhamer. "Archaeology at the Parvin Homestead: Searching for the Material Legacy of the Underground Railroad." *Historical Archaeology* 42, no. 2 (2008): 38–62. jstor.org/stable/25617495?seq=1.

Densmore, Christopher. "Quakers and the Underground Railroad: Myths and Realities." Quakers & Slavery. web.tricolib.brynmawr.edu/speccoll/quakersandslavery/commentary/organizations/underground_railroad.php.

Eschner, Kat. "When Enslaved People Commandeered a Ship and Hightailed It to Freedom in the Bahamas." *Smithsonian Magazine,* November 7, 2017. smithsonianmag.com/smart -news/slave-revolt-ended-128-enslaved-people-free -bahamas-180967070.

Estes, Adam Clark. "Thanks to 'Lincoln,' Mississippi Has Finally, Definitely Ratified the Thirteenth Amendment." *Atlantic,* February 17, 2013. theatlantic.com/politics/archive/2013/02 /thanks-lincoln-mississippi-has-finally-ratified-thirteenth -amendment/318248.

Fling, Sarah. "The Formerly Enslaved Household of the Grant Family." White House Historical Association, April 17, 2020. whitehousehistory.org/the-formerly-enslaved-household-of -the-grant-family.

Florida Museum. "Fort Mose: America's Black Colonial Fortress of Freedom." floridamuseum.ufl.edu/histarch/research /st-augustine/fort-mose.

Foner, Eric. *Gateway to Freedom: The Hidden History of the Underground Railroad.* New York: W. W. Norton, 2015.

Foner, Eric. *Nothing But Freedom: Emancipation and Its Legacy.* Baton Rouge: Louisiana State University Press, 1983.

Fornal, Justin. "Inside the Quest to Return Nat Turner's Skull to His Family." *National Geographic,* October 6, 2016. nationalgeographic.com/news/2016/10/nat-turner-skull-slave -rebellion-uprising.

Fort Mose Historical Society. "Community of Freedom!: The Fort Mose Story." fortmose.org/about-fort-mose.

Gara, Larry. *The Liberty Line: The Legend of the Underground Railroad.* Lexington: University Press of Kentucky, 1996.

Gara, Larry. "The Underground Railroad: Legend or Reality?" *Proceedings of the American Philosophical Society* 105, no. 3 (1961): 334–339. jstor.org/stable/985459?seq=1.

Gara, Larry. "William Still and the Underground Railroad." *Pennsylvania History: A Journal of Mid-Atlantic Studies* 28, no. 1 (January 1961): 33–44. jstor.org/stable/27770004.

Gates, Henry Louis, Jr. *The Classic Slave Narratives.* New York: New American Library, 2016.

Gates, Henry Louis, Jr., and Donald Yacovone. *The African Americans: Many Rivers to Cross.* Carlsbad, CA: Smiley Books, 2013.

Glesner, Anthony Patrick. "Laura Haviland: Neglected Heroine of the Underground Railroad." *Michigan Historical Review* 21, no. 1 (Spring 1995): 19–48. jstor.org/stable/20173491.

Goodheart, Adam. "The Secret History of the Underground Railroad." *Atlantic,* March 2015. theatlantic.com/magazine/archive/2015/03/the-secret-history-of-the-underground-railroad/384966.

Grant, Richard. "Deep in the Swamps, Archaeologists Are Finding How Fugitive Slaves Kept Their Freedom." *Smithsonian Magazine,* September 2016. smithsonianmag.com/history/deep-swamps-archaeologists-fugitive-slaves-kept-freedom-180960122.

Hagedorn, Ann. *Beyond the River: The Untold Story of the Heroes of the Underground Railroad.* New York: Simon & Schuster, 2004.

Hahn, Steven. *A Nation Under Our Feet: Black Political Struggles in the Rural South from Slavery to the Great Migration.* Cambridge, MA: Belknap, 2003.

Humez, Jean M. *Harriet Tubman: The Life and Life Stories.* Madison: University of Wisconsin Press, 2004.

Johnson, Walter. *Soul by Soul: Life Inside the Antebellum Slave Market.* Cambridge, MA: Harvard University Press, 1999.

Kammen, Carol. "On Doing Local History: The Underground Railroad and Local History." *History News* 54, no. 2 (Spring 1999): 3–4. jstor.org/stable/42655578.

Kane, Sean. "Myths & Understandings: Grant as a Slaveholder." American Civil War Museum, November 21, 2017. acwm.org /blog/myths-misunderstandings-grant-slaveholder.

Kerber, Linda. "Abolitionists and Amalgamators: The New York City Race Riots of 1834." *New York History* 48, no. 1 (January 1967): 28–39. jstor.org/stable/23162902.

LaRoche, Cheryl Janifer. *Free Black Communities and the Underground Railroad: The Geography of Resistance.* Urbana: University of Illinois Press, 2014.

Larson, Kate Clifford. *Bound for the Promised Land: Harriet Tubman, Portrait of an American Hero.* New York: One World, 2004.

Law, Robin. *The Slave Coast of West Africa 1550–1750: The Impact of the Atlantic Slave Trade on an African Society.* Oxford: Clarendon, 1991.

Lincoln, Abraham. *The Collected Works of Abraham Lincoln.* Vol. 2. Edited by Roy P. Basler. New Brunswick, NJ: Rutgers University Press, 1953.

Masur, Jenny. "Building a National Underground Railroad Network to Freedom." *Practicing Anthropology* 26, no. 1 (Winter 2004): 31–35. jstor.org/stable/24781510.

National Museum of African American History & Culture. "The Underground Railroad." nmaahc.si.edu/blog/underground -railroad.

National Park Service. "Myths & Facts About Harriet Tubman." Harriet Tubman Underground Railroad Byway. nps.gov/hatu /planyourvisit/upload/MD_TubmanFactSheet_MythsFacts_2 .pdf.

New England Historical Society. "Lewis Hayden, the Kentucky Fugitive Who Fled Slavery." newenglandhistoricalsociety.com /lewis-hayden-kentucky-fugitive-left-behind-slavery.

PBS. "The Underground Railroad." Africans in America. pbs.org /wgbh/aia/part4/4p2944.html.

Price, Richard. "Maroons: Rebel Slaves in the Americas." Center for Folklife and Cultural Heritage of the Smithsonian Institution. folklife.si.edu/resources/maroon/educational_guide/23.htm.

Rediker, Marcus. *The Slave Ship: A Human History.* New York: Viking, 2007.

Richardson, Marilyn, ed. *Maria W. Stewart, America's First Black Woman Political Writer: Essays and Speeches.* Bloomington: Indiana University Press, 1987.

"Runaway Slaves." *New York Times*, November 26, 1852.
timesmachine.nytimes.com/timesmachine/1852/11/26
/75122013.pdf?pdf_redirect=true&ip=0.

Still, William. *The Underground Railroad Records: Narrating the
Hardships, Hairbreadth Escapes, and Death Struggles of Slaves in
Their Efforts for Freedom.* Edited by Quincy T. Mills. New York:
Modern Library, 2019.

Strother, Horatio T. *The Underground Railroad in Connecticut.*
Middletown, CT: Wesleyan University Press, 1962.

Stukin, Stacie. "Unravelling the Myths of Quilts and the Underground
Railroad." *Time*, April 3, 2007. content.time.com/time/arts
/article/0,8599,1606271,00.html.

Thomas, Hugh. *The Slave Trade: The Story of the Transatlantic Slave
Trade: 1440–1870.* New York: Simon & Schuster, 1997.

Underground Railroad History Project. "Stephen and Harriet Myers
Residence: Past, Present and Future."
undergroundrailroadhistory.org/residence.

US Congress. Commission to Study and Develop Reparation Proposals
for African-Americans Act. H.R. 40, 116th Congress, January 3,
2019. congress.gov/bill/116th-congress/house-bill/40.

Virginia Humanities. "Runaway Servants (1643)." *Encyclopedia
Virginia.* encyclopediavirginia.org/entries/runaway
-servants-1643.

Wellman, Judith. "The Underground Railroad and the National
Register of Historic Places: Historical Importance vs.
Architectural Integrity." *Public Historian* 24, no. 1 (Winter 2002):
11–29. jstor.org/stable/10.1525/tph.2002.24.1.11?seq=1.

IMAGE CREDITS

INDEX

SMASH MORE STORIES!

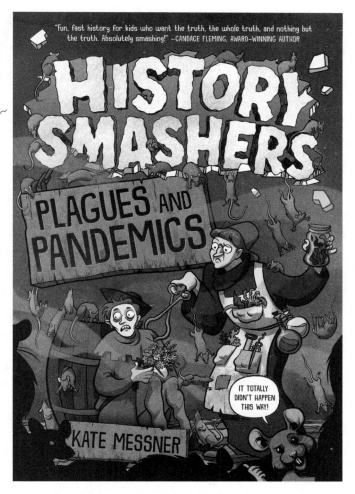

"Fun, fast history for kids who want the truth, the whole truth, and nothing but the truth. Absolutely smashing!" —CANDACE FLEMING, AWARD-WINNING AUTHOR

HISTORY SMASHERS

PLAGUES AND PANDEMICS

IT TOTALLY DIDN'T HAPPEN THIS WAY!

KATE MESSNER

TURN THE PAGE FOR A SNEAK PEEK AT ANOTHER GREAT BOOK IN THE HISTORY SMASHERS SERIES!

You've probably heard about the Black Death and other big disease outbreaks in history. If you're reading this book, you've probably even lived through one yourself.

Widespread outbreaks of illnesses make history because they can alter populations, power structures, and government policies. They've taught us about science and changed the way we deal with everything from throwing away garbage to preventing disease and caring for the sick.

But some of the stories told about outbreaks are just plain wrong. A long time ago, people were certain that diseases were caused by angry gods or bad-smelling air. If you were sick, friends might advise you to drink wine or eat crushed emeralds. If those cures didn't work, you might have tried putting pig bladders full of hot water under your armpits!

Thankfully, most of those way-off-base remedies are a thing of the past. Today, we know that many diseases are caused by tiny organisms known as microbes, such as bacteria and viruses. And today, most people—but not all—listen to science instead of myths when it comes to understanding illnesses and treatments. Still, the history of plagues and pandemics is full of stories that need smashing, starting with ancient times and continuing through today. So let's get to work. . . .

ONE
ANCIENT AILMENTS

Microbes have been around a lot longer than people, and they'll probably be around well after we're gone. Most microbes are harmless or beneficial. They help us digest food and fight off infection. But microbes can also make us sick.

When lots of people get sick from the same microbe at the same time, that's called an epidemic.

When an epidemic spreads around the world, it's called a pandemic.

The first recorded epidemics in history go all the way back to ancient times. *The Epic of Gilgamesh,* a poem written in ancient Mesopotamia, mentioned a visit from the god of pestilence (disease) around 2000 BCE. Ancient Egyptian and Chinese writings also refer to pestilence.

One of the first well-documented epidemics was the Plague of Athens, which happened in 430 BCE. The Greek city-state of Athens was fighting Sparta in the Peloponnesian War, and Athens had built walls around the city. People from the countryside moved inside to be protected, creating a super-crowded place where disease could spread easily.

A general and historian named Thucydides wrote that a quarter of the Athenian army died. What made them sick? We don't know, because people didn't understand diseases well at that time, but we can make some guesses based on ancient writings.

Fortunately, Thucydides himself got sick! While this was rotten news for him, it was good news for modern scientists and historians who have tried to piece together what happened in Athens. These are the symptoms Thucydides wrote down:

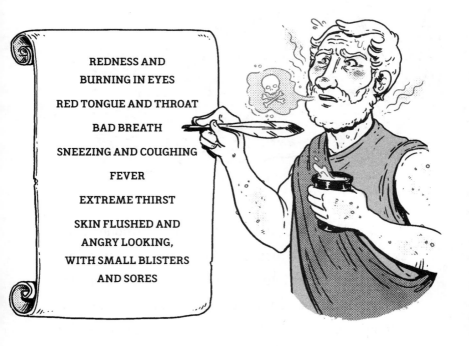

REDNESS AND
BURNING IN EYES

RED TONGUE AND THROAT

BAD BREATH

SNEEZING AND COUGHING

FEVER

EXTREME THIRST

SKIN FLUSHED AND
ANGRY LOOKING,
WITH SMALL BLISTERS
AND SORES

"*Internally it burned so that the patient could not bear to have on him clothing or linen even of the very lightest description; or indeed to be otherwise than stark naked. What they would have liked best would have been to throw themselves into cold water, as indeed was done by some of the neglected sick, who plunged into the rain-tanks in their agonies of unquenchable thirst.*"

—THUCYDIDES, *HISTORY OF THE PELOPONNESIAN WAR*

Based on the list of symptoms, modern-day experts think the disease might have been smallpox or measles. Even though it's called the Plague of Athens, they don't think it's likely that people had bubonic plague, because that disease produces big bulges on the body, called buboes, which would have been hard for old Thucydides to ignore in his descriptions. Whatever it was, the epidemic devastated Athens, which lost the war. It was the beginning of the end for what had been the most powerful city-state in Greece . . . all because of a microbe, a tiny germ that no one could even see.

THE MUMMIES HAD MALARIA

Some of ancient Egypt's disease history is recorded in the bodies of preserved mummies. Around 6000 BCE, when people started farming in Egypt, they noticed that the Nile River flooded once a year, swamping the valley on both sides. The flooding was great for creating fertile soil for crops, but it was also perfect for mosquitoes, which breed in standing, shallow water. Mosquitoes can carry a tiny parasite that causes a disease we now call malaria.

In 1922, archaeologist Howard Carter opened the inner shrine of the tomb of King Tutankhamen, better known as King Tut. Scientists now believe the king had malaria before he died at age nineteen.

Papyrus scrolls written by doctors in ancient Egypt talk about "the pest of the year," an illness that showed up when the river flooded. Was it malaria? Thousands of years later, some well-preserved mummies still held the answer to that question. Archaeologists studied a group of mummies from one area of Egypt and found that almost half of them showed evidence of being infected with malaria.

The more people travel, the more diseases can spread. As ancient trade routes opened up, microbes hitched a ride on ships and caravans carrying silk and spices. And when armies traveled during wartime, their crowded camps were a perfect breeding ground for bacteria and viruses.

Back then people didn't know what was making them sick. The ancient Greeks blamed angry gods and believed that if you were ill, you needed to patch things up with the gods so they'd make you well again. So they built asclepeions, which were sort of half shrines and half hospitals where sick people could go to ask priests for help with cures. Asclepeions were located in pretty country settings with clean air and pure water, and people who went there were encouraged to eat a healthy diet, exercise, and get lots of rest. Those practices were probably why some of the sick got better—not because the priests there had some sort of direct line to the gods.

If you think being treated at an asclepeion sounds pretty great, there's one more thing you should know: one of the cures involved having snakes slither over you. The snakes were considered sacred and could supposedly make people well . . . somehow.

The tradition came about because Asclepius, the god of medicine and healing, was often pictured with a serpent curled around his staff. This snake imagery is still connected to medicine today; both the American Medical Association (AMA) and the World Health Organization (WHO) have serpents on their logos.

Later on in ancient Greece, people wondered if something other than angry gods might be making people sick. A philosopher named Aristotle suggested that the world was made up of four elements— earth, water, air, and fire. He and his students also thought the human body contained four fluids called humors—black bile, phlegm, blood, and yellow bile— and if these humors got out of balance somehow, they made a person sick.

That explanation wasn't quite right, of course, and it led to some questionable treatments. If doctors thought you had too much blood, they'd just slice you open with a sharp tool called a lancet to get rid of some. This treatment, called bloodletting, persisted for thousands of years. In fact, America's first president, George Washington, was bled right before he died in 1799. He'd come down with a fever, and doctors thought bleeding him might help. (Spoiler: It didn't.)

Even though the ancient Greeks got a lot wrong, the idea that diseases were caused by something natural was a starting place. Once doctors understood that, they could test different theories to learn more.

HISTORY SMASHERS

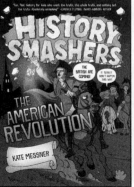

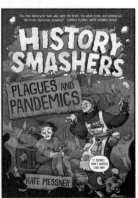